THE BEST COUNTRY
Why Canada Will Lead the Future

THE
BEST COUNTRY

Why Canada Will Lead the Future

For Donna
Best Wishes

Satya Das

Canadian Cataloguing in Publication Data
National Library of Canada Cataloguing in Publication

Das, Satya, 1955-
The best country

ISBN 0-9731134-0-5

1. Canada--Emigration and immigration. 2. Peacekeeping forces--Canada. 3. Canada--Foreign relations--1945- I. Title.

| FC635.D37 2002 | 971.064'8 | C2002-910661-3 |
| F1034.2.D373 2002 | | |

Editor: Don Kerr
Copy Editor: Peter Adler
Design: Ruth Linka
Cover image: Calvin Caldwell
Author photo: Mita Das

Every effort has been made to obtain permission for quoted material. If there is an omission or error the author and publisher would be grateful to be so informed.

Published by Sextant, an imprint of Cambridge Strategies Inc.

Cambridge Strategies Inc.
Suite 208, 10080 Jasper Avenue
Edmonton, Alberta
T5J 1V9
www.cambridgestrategies.com

1 2 3 4 5 05 04 03 02

PRINTED AND BOUND IN CANADA

To my parents, who led me to a clear understanding

You must be the change you wish to see in the world
~ Mohandas Karamchand Gandhi

And at dawn, with ardent patience,
we shall enter cities of splendour
(Et à l'aurore, armés d'une ardente patience,
nous entrerons aux splendides villes)
~ Arthur Rimbaud

CONTENTS

ACKNOWLEDGEMENTS

ON THE LAST DAY OF THE OLD MILLENNIUM, I LEFT BEHIND a quarter century in journalism to embark on a life as a writer. I could not have abandoned the certainty of a comfortable existence without the support of my family: my wife Mita and my daughters Silpi and Somya. They are my *raison d'être*, and I am forever grateful for their confidence and their love. I am especially thankful to them and to our extended families for their patience and understanding throughout the making of *The Best Country*.

The Best Country would have been a lesser book but for the wise and patient counsel of my editor Don Kerr. I thank him for his intellectual rigour, and his insistence in challenging and testing my central arguments. Andy Knight's final crafting produced a far better work, as did Peter Adler's tenacious copy-editing. Many other friends and colleagues contributed to the development of these arguments, and I am grateful for their generosity.

Many voices and ideas shape a book. My ideas are bound to the thoughts and teachings of several philosophers: Siddhartha Gautama, Socrates, Ramanuja, Nicoló Machiavelli, François-Marie Arouet, Jean-Jacques Rousseau and above all Mohandas Karamchand Gandhi, who continues to light the way.

Any errors or omissions are my own.

Satya Das, Edmonton

A MATTER OF DESTINY

When the Aga Khan declared Canada a prototype for the world in February 2002, he spoke a truth many of us know in our hearts. The spiritual leader of the world's Ismaili Muslims, many of whom were welcomed in Canada after they were expelled from East Africa in the 1970s, was not merely expressing gratitude. He wanted to tell Canadians, during his visit to our country, that what we have is singular in the human experience: a nation where people from the world over construct a common life and a common destiny.

Sometimes it takes an outsider to say what we do not, to acknowledge the Canada that is a model for the human family. Indeed, we Canadians are so wedded to our traditional modesty that we feel more comfortable in the shadows than in the spotlight. When Canada slipped to third place in the United Nations Human Development Index in 2001, there seemed to be as many expressions of relief as of regret. It was, as one politician told me, a return to "reality," a welcome release from the notion that Canada was the best country in the world. Yet, the story of how Canada became the best country, dominating the United Nations rankings ever since the Human Development Index launched in 1993, deserves deeper and more careful exploration than the media snippets that accompany the annual rankings.

Despite the reluctance in some quarters to acknowledge Canada's grand achievement of the 1990s – an entirely expected result of typically Canadian diffidence, if not deference – it is worth reflecting on how the United Nations ranking came to be. The Human Development Index is a basket of diverse measurements such as life expectancy, infant mortality, educational standards, pay equity, and the instance of children in poverty[1]. Nations are ranked according to their progress on all of these scales, and an overall ranking is taken by combining national standings in all of these measures. In essence, the HDI is a measure of a country's standard of civilisation; of how a nation ranks in the quality of life it offers its citizens. Each year the methodology is improved and refined, as the Index strives to bring some rigour to the subjective criterion suggested by the phrases "quality of life" and "civil society."

Indeed, in its groundbreaking 2000 report, the United Nations explicitly linked HDI ranking with the advancement of human rights, human development and human security – three overlapping and interlinked concepts that are the core of an alternative vision of the world. While these phenomena are explored in some detail in later chapters, it should be noted that – taken together – they amount to a new way of looking at the world, particularly with regard to the evolution of civil society and notions of global governance. Rather than an international order predicated on relationships between nations, this model goes beyond political boundaries to advocate the wellbeing of the individual citizen, no matter where she lives. Human rights implies freedom from fear, and threats to one's fundamental existence. Human development asserts a claim to the resources and freedoms one needs to develop to one's full potential. And human security evokes freedom from hunger, war, ecological disaster, corrupt governance and other impediments to a life lived in justice, with equality of opportunity for all. This vision departs from those notions of nation-states guaranteeing security by building significant military capacity, and using economic prowess to secure their own prosperity with scant regard for the progress of others.

The UN said in its 2000 Human Development Report: "If human development focuses on the enhancement of the capabilities and freedoms that the members of a community enjoy, human rights represent the claims that individuals have on the conduct of individual and collective agents and on the design of social arrangements to facilitate or secure these capabilities and freedoms."

It went on to note that: "An adequate conception of human development cannot ignore the importance of political liberties and democratic freedoms. Indeed, democratic freedom and civil rights can be extremely important for enhancing the capabilities of people who are poor. They can do this directly, since poor people have strong reason to resist abuse and exploitation by their employers and politicians. And they can do this indirectly, since those who hold power have political incentives to respond to acute deprivations when the deprived can make use of their political freedom to protest, criticise and oppose."

If a high standard of civilisation depends upon the advancement of human rights, human security and human development, then Canada can rightly assert that the world ought not to be driven by economic globalisation alone. If we are indeed the best country, then we will lead the future by working in that more complex sphere where society, culture, politics and economics intersect. *The Best Country: Why Canada Will Lead the Future* does not aim to tell a chronological or scholarly story of how Canada came to top the HDI. Rather, it invites Canadians to consider some of the forces and currents that brought us to this stature, and to consider the implications of what that standing means. We need to remember how we came to be, how we acquired the esteem in which we are held. And in the sometimes stark choice between the headlong pursuit of economic gain and the pursuit of a more equitable world founded on notions of human security, we need to acknowledge that the latter agenda is more in keeping with Canada's traditions and values. Moreover, it has made the more substantial contribution to Canada's ranking as the world's leading civil society. Indeed, there is no simple or straightforward correlation between economic prowess and quality of life. As measured by the World Bank's Purchasing Power Parity formula (free of the artificial influence of currency exchange rates), the world's four largest economies in 2000 were the United States, China, Japan and India. In that year, those countries ranked third, 99th, ninth and 128th respectively on the Human Development Index. Canada, which ranked atop the HDI in 2000, was the 12th largest economy, just behind Mexico, on the World Bank measurement.

Indeed, a look at the top ten rankings in both 2000 and 2001 HDI shows a high correlation between the advancement of human rights and human development, as well as sound economic performance; the World Bank economic rankings in themselves do not necessarily reflect an adherence to a high quality of life.[2]

This is not to say we are perfect, or that we are close to perfect. No country is. And the United Nations Universal Declaration of Human Rights sets such a standard that it might be a very long time before anyone comes close to fulfilling all the ideals therein. We should recognise, however, that our top ranking gives us the legitimacy to make the projection of Canadian values abroad something other than an act of presumption and arrogance. We should not downplay what Canada's standing means: our model of civil society is the highest standard of civilisation achieved by any nation in the world.

Canadians need to come to grips with their achievement because we are in a better position to influence the conduct of statecraft and international relations. In the early months of this new century, the question of whether Canada or Australia or Norway led the HDI did not necessarily enjoy much relevancy in the *realpolitik* world of nuclear-armed states and a rapacious form of economic globalisation that benefited the few at the expense of the many. Yet the terrorist attack on the United States on 11 September 2001 shook that world to the core. Even as the United States launched a police action against those it presumed responsible for the outrage, its citizens indulged in introspection and reflection about the nature of the world, and their nation's place therein.

In this search to give substance and meaning to the "kinder, gentler nation" Americans were once promised, the example of Canada and Canadianism gain a new dimension. Rather than being ignored and taken for granted, Canada is seen in America's leadership elite as that country's intimate friend, even a member of the family, for standing shoulder to shoulder in a time of shock and grief. This new-found perspective gives Canada a substantial opportunity to lead and influence the shaping of a civil world.

We should begin with an acknowledgement that we have an obligation to lead. The Canadian penchant for hiding our light under a bushel, ducking our heads when we are praised, standing aside to follow in the footsteps of the more confident and more powerful, simply will not do. Like it or not, the quality of our civilisation gives us an obligation to share our experience with the other peoples in the world, to offer the example of a national space wherein the peoples of the world can coexist and flourish. The aftermath of the 11 September 2001 attacks, with a new emphasis on fighting the root causes of terror, gives us the ideal opening to exercise benign influence on the United States.

All those who vented a sigh of relief when Canada dropped to third cannot slough off so easily the burden of leadership, nor take comfort in a single year's ranking. In the decade since the creation of the Human Development Index, Canada has held second place once, third place once, and first place eight times, including seven straight years from 1994-2000.

And in the age of fighting the sources of terrorism, by bringing hope and choice and responsibility to people oppressed and manipulated by totalitarian regimes, this primacy is particularly important. Once the guns stop and the arduous task of rebuilding a viable society begins, Canada has an obligation to lead the movement beyond the confines of economic globalisation, to that sphere where society, culture, economics and politics all intermingle and intersect. We know that that answer to terrorism lies not just in police action against perpetrators, but in creating a more civil and more secure world, where the benefits and the opportunities of human civilisation are available far more broadly than they have been.

Before the Sept. 11 attacks, it was clear economic globalisation is a reality. But it is no longer an article of blind faith, advanced with the triumphal belief that the power of economic development and growth will lift all boats like a rising tide. The aftermath of the attacks drew attention to the example of many nations where economics alone has not proven to be a panacea. The terrorist attack, coupled with the spectacular collapse of Enron, abruptly ended the aura of invincibility and invulnerability that had become the hallmark of American civilisation. Indeed, Enron offered a telling example of what happens when market forces are unleashed without let or hindrance. The energy trading company that built its empire on high-risk ventures beyond the ambit of weak and deficient regulations became a monopoly that acted as buyer and seller, the indispensable conduit for those who produced and those who consumed. The entire scripture of thug capitalism – the credo of "get government out of the way and let business do what it does best" – was born in the Reagan years and nourished in the last two decades of the 20th century. It fuelled the creation of a world without economic borders, where the flow of capital would erase all regulatory obstacles or attempts at scrutiny. The fantasy that a state can secure its borders to make itself invincible, and enable its businesses to use that safe haven to expand without limit, had become an article of faith in the US and indeed much of the developed world before Sept. 11 and Enron. It flew in the face of pervasive evidence of globalisation, not just in economics, but in many other spheres. Yet globalisation often seemed a theoretical construct rather than a reality of life, until that terrible day.

In the months after the attacks, we are reminded in the most harrowing way that no country can afford the illusion that it is able to hide behind its borders, pretending that the outside world does not exist. Economic globalisation has made the world borderless, by extending the power and reach of the marketplace across national boundaries into every part of the globe. Now we know that terrorism too is without borders, a brutal reminder that the world cannot be run by economics alone. If economic globalisation is borderless, so is terror. So is ecological degradation. So is smuggling. So is drug trafficking and prostitution. The challenge then is, can we make opportunity borderless? Can we offer the most wretched of the world some semblance of the life that the most privileged take for granted?

We need to give due consideration of every aspect of society and culture, if the benefits of a borderless world are to go beyond economics so they can be extended to a far greater proportion of the world's people. Canada has made a good start with its doctrine of human security as the basis of its foreign policy. In contrast to the "free markets first" approach of economic panaceas, the human security agenda focuses on the building blocks of civil society. Its key principle – freedom from pervasive threats to people's lives or livelihood, be they political, social or economic – starts with the notion that human rights are indeed universal and indivisible. As the United Nations made clear in its 2000 Human Development Report, the extension of this rights-based approach around the world is the only long-term guarantor of a more peaceful and more equitable world. This is admittedly a controversial notion, vigorously resisted by those who value borders and traditional concepts of the nation-state. Yet that is precisely why the Human Development Report amounted to a pioneering document – it brought into sharp focus the difference between traditional notions of global governance and the emerging creed of human rights, human security and human development as the most desirable basis of relations between countries and peoples. All three of those depend on a strong foundation of economic development and equitable access to economic opportunity and resources. And that same report made clear that the HDI is also a measure of how robustly a country practises the culture of human rights. By conferring that honourable mantle upon Canada, it also sets the stage for where Canada must lead if we are to take globalisation beyond mere economics.

We need the globalisation of human rights.

We need the globalisation of peace.

We need the globalisation of education.

We need the globalisation of health care.

We need to globalise equal opportunity for all.

And we as Canadians need to lead this expansion of what globalisation means. We need to fulfil the obligation of leadership, because that is the duty of the best country in the world. Of all of these, the most important is the globalisation of human rights. Human rights are ultimately the foundation of civil society, and without them, no society can truly flourish, no matter how rich its economy. The root of this freedom is non-violence, the grand concept championed by M.K. Gandhi and followed so effectively by Martin Luther King, Nelson Mandela, and the Dalai Lama. In its essence, non-violence is the freedom to be safe.

That is also the measure at the heart of the Human Development Index (HDI), and it is by this measure that Canada's civil society has come to lead the world.

This leadership flows not only from Canadians concerned about social justice, but can also come from our businesses and enterprises. It comes not just from our politicians, but also from those thoughtful Canadians who take to the streets to voice well-founded concerns about the dangers of enabling a world in which the pursuit of economic power is paramount.

At the Summit of the Americas in April 2001, 23-year-old Eileen Kilgour joined thousands of other young Canadians on the barricaded streets of Quebec City, demanding that the civil society and culture of peace we take for granted in Canada be extended to every nation in the hemisphere.

9

"This summit represented another example of the people being left out of the debate," she observed. "The Free Trade Agreement of the Americas was discussed behind a large wall while the people in the street were left outside. Free Trade has many negative attributes that need to be regulated in order for the system to work fairly. We need to look more critically at how free trade affects people's lives and our environment. This cannot be done if civil society is left out of the decision-making process."

She wandered into a protesting crowd as police fired tear gas, made common cause with young people from all over Canada and the world, and noted: "Many individuals feel frustrated over the lack of participation in our governmental system and the many inequalities that exist in our world. The current system gives too much power to large corporations, governments in power and the capitalist system that has created a developed and a developing world. We need to work towards a system where equality, the rights of all people and the environment come first."

Her cogent summation captures a missing part of the dialogue about the role and place of Canada in shaping the future, a voice that is likely to be heard more clearly in the world changed by the events of 11 September 2001.

Eileen recalls Saturday evening at the summit, following an afternoon when Black Bloc anarchists who had infiltrated the crowds led organised assaults on the fence and on the massed police. "Later that evening, the city called a state of emergency and I was still downtown. I sat under the bridge at a safe area that was serving free food and watched as the police moved on the protesters. I was feeling so ill from the tear gas that I went back to the University of Laval where thousands of people were sleeping on the floor. There were a total of about 100 students from my university who went to Quebec City. One of my friends stood on the wall and was teargassed for hours, another was part of the blue group that would go in every area and bring help to anyone who needed it, others ripped down the wall, and others watched or photographed what they saw. I was in the green group committed to no violence. On Sunday, I was involved with the Earth Day activities that were being put on by the Sierra Club. I attended three lectures on the environmental consequences of Free Trade and then helped with the clean-up of the city. The clean-up received much positive attention; many Quebec City citizens even came up to us and wanted to know what we were doing. We explained to them that it was Earth Day and we wanted to clean up their city for hosting us. We even got a round of applause by a van full of police officers. It was a refreshing contrast to the previous day where I only saw anger from both sides."

What makes Eileen's story unusual, apart from her gift of vividly conveying her experiences, is that her father was on the other side of the barricade, behind the overwhelming police presence protecting a more official version of "democracy." He was part of a large delegation of Canadians inside the meeting hall, trying to inject human rights and democracy into a largely economic agenda. Eileen's father David was at the time Canada's Secretary of State for Latin America and Africa. "We were both trying to accomplish the same goals," remarks David. "Without the pressure from the young people outside, I'm not certain we would have been able to get agreement in principle on the Democracy Charter, which was later passed unanimously by a special assembly of the OAS in Lima, Peru – approximately one hour after those planes hit the World Trade Center."

Eileen recalls, "My most important contribution in Quebec City was being an educated, critical, non-violent citizen who wanted to be involved in the process. I wanted to better understand the globalisation movement and Canada's role within free trade. The Summit highlighted that there is much mistrust in our current system. Instead of a valuable debate, I saw anger and frustration. The media furthered this situation by portraying only the violence and the clash between the police and the protesters."

Eileen's analysis reflects a view of political engagement and political activism that is difficult to capture in the narrow confines of political parties. Her political consciousness, and the convictions of the young people she describes, go beyond the traditional conflicts of partisan strife – their motives and inspirations are too broad to fit into the templates of partisan political discourse by which most democracies organise representative government. It reflects a consensus that opposes an established order, but does not use the tradition of partisan politics that shaped and governs the established order. This phenomenon is part of what I propose to call The Demotic Society – a notion and a theme that is explored in more substance in later chapters.

The experiences of a daughter and a father, each pursuing a Canadian tradition of trying to craft a more just and equitable global society, offer a small illustration of how Canada can lead the future. Our national government's commitment to using human security, as the foundation of all foreign policy, is a remarkably enlightened step. As defined by the Ministry of Foreign Affairs, where David now serves as Canada's Secretary of State for Asia, the human security agenda puts civil rights above all other interests: "Canada's human security agenda responds to new global realities. Its goal is to ensure that people can live in freedom from fear. This means building a world where universal humanitarian standards and the rule of law effectively protect all people; where those who violate these standards and laws are held accountable; and where our global, regional and bilateral institutions are equipped to defend and enforce these standards. As Canadians, we are committed to working with like-minded partners, at home and abroad, to build this world."

In the foreign policy document *Freedom from Fear*, David's ministry notes: "In 1996, when Canada first outlined human security as 'protection for civilians' at the UN General Assembly, the concept was little understood or accepted. Four years later, during Canada's April 2000 presidency of the Security Council, the language of human security was well established. As a result of Canada's initiative, the Security Council agenda has come to include issues such as protecting civilians in armed conflict, reforming sanctions regimes, changing and fine-tuning the conditions under which sanctions are imposed. The goal is to reduce their humanitarian costs, defending the rights of women in places such as Afghanistan, and addressing the need to intervene on behalf of civilians to prevent a future Rwanda or Srebrenica."

The concept of human security, advocated robustly by United Nations Secretary General Kofi Annan, may become a vital element in Canada's obligation to lead the journey to a better future for all humankind. Citing Czech President Vaclav Havel's observation that "The sovereignty of the community, the region, the nation, the state . . . makes sense only if it is derived from the one genuine sovereignty – that is, from the sovereignty of the human being," the federal government notes in *Freedom from Fear*, "the concept of peace and security – national, regional and global – makes sense only if it is derived from individual security. This perspective informs Canadian foreign policy today. This is what we mean by human security."

Using human security as a foundation, both David's generation and Eileen's can indeed share common cause, in advancing forms of globalisation that go well beyond economics, and the seemingly insatiable demands of predatory capitalism. We know that enlightened capitalism flows from civil society and a strong foundation of democracy, transparency and accountability. If the market economy is to work, it must be accompanied by the globalisation of the forces and influences that temper the uncontrolled excesses of capitalism. When Alberta Energy Company bought an oil company in Ecuador, it began to apply Canadian-style ecological protection – much to the amusement of its competitors, including the state-owned oil company which continued to dump 40,000 litres of oily brine a day into the headwaters of the Amazon River. International Nickel met similar puzzlement when it embarked on a copper mine in Indonesia – building schools, health clinics, and community centres. These were "bare minimum" investments by Canadian standards, yet were seen as exceptional by local ones. Applying common standards in all free trade treaties, for instance, would create a level playing field – workers would enjoy a better life, and there would be less of a race to the bottom by investors chasing the places with the least amount of environmental and labour regulation. The advancement of civil society and the pursuit of profit need not be mutually exclusive goals. Why not export Canada's model of civil society to countries that need it and can make use of it by adapting it to their own cultural and societal experience?

Our traders would rather export wheat or oil or technology, and as a nation it sometimes appears that we would rather sell nuclear reactors than civil rights. Yet if we are to develop a comprehensive brand-image to sell Canada with all its strengths, to help our international trade and commerce, we need to get beyond the business-first mindset, to describe our country warts and all. A clear-sighted examination of our past will make the Canadian story all the more remarkable. We can explain to our international partners that Canada's civil society is special because we have had our share of wrongdoing and injustice. Our present-day accommodation of cultural and racial diversity is all the more remarkable given our past of head taxes, forced internment and the subjugation and deracination of aboriginal peoples and cultures. Our ability to build consensus, to find an evolving national identity, to establish a context for peace, order and good government to flourish have all evolved from a shameful and horrific past. That's why the great Canadian experiment – the task of building a nation from every imaginable stream of human experience – can be a fine model for the world. We are at last engaged in the arduous endeavour of coming to terms with the injustice once bred in the bone; we are at last beginning to address past wrongs and present shortcomings. There are setbacks, like British Columbia Premier Gordon Campbell's corrosive referendum on aboriginal property rights, and the socio-economic status of Canada's First Nations remains far below that of the general population. Yet even as Canada strives to improve, it must be noted that many countries in the world haven't yet come to the point where they can admit they have terrible wrongs that need to be fixed.

Amnesty International's campaign to highlight human rights abuses in the United States is meeting both indignation and denial. Yet most Canadians can see there are social and racial issues in the US that might better be addressed using Canada's social model. Racial tensions in Britain and France – the two principal sources of Canada's non-aboriginal identity – have not been overcome despite many well-intentioned interventions, largely because neither of those countries is willing to expand its national identity enough to accommodate newcomers. The help our democratic allies need is of course minimal compared with many of the nastier countries of the world. Canada is a pioneer in the new frontier territory of peace building, of creating civil society where none exists.

We share a common agenda with United Nations Secretary General Kofi Annan, one that has evolved in a continuum in the Canadian Foreign Service from Lester Pearson to Joe Clark to Lloyd Axworthy – and this is a pioneering endeavour in which we can justly take some satisfaction, notwithstanding the enormity of the task. We are perhaps better placed to be the Secretary General's leading partners in this vital human endeavour because of our national character. Canada's unique strength, the ability to accommodate many streams of culture and human experience within a dynamic and evolving national identity, will gain more importance as the world becomes ever more interlinked.

Canadians are well positioned, thanks to the HDI, to argue that the world should be built on a model of human security. That's not just a rhetorical flourish, it's the essential concept that must continue to drive public policy in Canada – there may be arguments over how costly or elaborate that model ought to be, but the broader concept of security is what animates the Canadian sense of civil society. Indeed, when Canada dropped to third place on the 2001 HDI Prime Minister Jean Chrétien pledged to do what was necessary to regain first place – to liberate so many First Nations Canadians from the Third World living conditions; to ease the grip of poverty in a time of plenty. Of course, critics such as Professor Tom Keating of the University of Alberta quite rightly note that Canada's noble rhetoric on human security and human rights has not been backed up by the requisite funding, that Canada is better at sounding noble (and ultimately hollow) than actually marshalling the resources to lend substance to its stated intent.

The reason we dropped to third was clear: we have not done nearly enough to address the persistence of poverty, nor have we addressed the growing gap between rich and poor both at home and in the world. It is by setting our domestic house in order – by ensuring that human rights, human dignity and human security are extended to all our citizens – that we will better prepare ourselves to assert global leadership in crafting a more civil world. No matter how un-Canadian it may appear to think of ourselves as exceptional, we must recognise that our country is singularly blessed. The alternative to exporting Canadian values and the Canadian model of civil society was made brutally clear on 11 September 2001. Building a culture of peace is the strongest possible response to a world where violence ascends, where terrorists fly aeroplanes into large public buildings, or stone six-year-old school children who belong to a different Christian sect.

The Best Country is not just a call for Canadian leadership. It also invites us to consider the inevitable prospect that we are destined to lead. If a world without borders is going to bring people, cultures and societies into closer and deeper contact, whether by benign intent or malevolent design, our world needs some assurance that all humans can indeed live together and flourish. If not our example, whose?

THE BEST COUNTRY

EVERY IMMIGRANT REMEMBERS THE ARRIVAL.

Barry remembers coming off a boat from New Zealand, to be met by a Vancouver immigration official who told him, "You'll never make it here, go back home."

Nizar and Razia remember the desperate escape from Idi Amin's Uganda, each fleeing separately: Razia arriving in Montreal with her 10-month old son in her arms, unsure where Nizar was, or "how I would find him again."

Nella remembers the Halifax docks at the end of the voyage from Italy, and the train that brought her family to Edmonton. "It seemed like the country kept on going forever."

Jan remembers arriving in Montreal, giddy with the sheer exhilaration of leaving communist era Poland and its stifling conventions, "I had nothing but I didn't care; it was so good just to breathe freely."

And I remember a grey April day at Vancouver airport, carrying the ridiculously warm parka my father had sent all the way to India, surveying everything with the agile curiosity of a boy beginning a new adventure.

Multiply us by the millions and you will find the makings of modern Canada. From many strands of the human experience, beginning with the migration of today's First Nations more than 12,000 years ago, we have woven the best country in the world.

This is no small accomplishment. Yet by and large we Canadians are reluctant to affirm that our status carries with it a responsibility, even a duty, to serve as a template for the new borderless world, the world of societies in transition, as the progress of the global economy and the communications revolution shatters the notion of borders between people, culture and nations. We are a national space where the entire world may flourish, because in this country there is room enough for everyone's dreams, and we are free to define our place in this vastness. We have seldom asserted the international leadership that our status confers.

～

Part of the immigrant impulse is to seek out a haven, a place that is safer and more appealing than the world left behind. We know Canada is more than a nation that defies the natural patterns of geography and commerce: it is the sum of our collective will, a collective act of faith in which decency and compassion and the best qualities of the human heart can find expression. It is no accident that this settler society, this country defined by a never-ending search for accommodation and consensus, has become the template for building a higher standard of civilisation.

In its post-war history, as the Aga Khan said, Canada has developed as a model for the world. Yet what is it about Canada that makes it work? How did it all come together? And is it always going to last? Only forty years ago, bilingualism was a gleam in someone's eye, and the idea of putting cultural diversity in the Constitution was a pipe dream. Medicare was still taking root, and the compassionate state was still a work in progress. Many schools still had the strap. The sins of our public history – the treatment of Ukrainian Canadians in the First World War and Japanese Canadians in the second; the legacy of decades of cultural annihilation of aboriginal Canadians – had yet to be acknowledged, let alone atoned. English was still very much the dominant language of the Quebec economy; a francophone Quebecer in her home province had to learn English to have any chance at advancement.

To convey the sense of transformation in our country, let's capture two golden moments: the Olympic ice hockey championships won by Canada's men's and women's teams at the 2002 Salt Lake City games. Canada won because Haley Wickenheiser's ancestors came from Germanic Europe, Cassie Campbell's from the British Isles and Therese Brisson's from France. Canada won because Wayne Gretzky's grandfather fled Belarus. Canada's men's team scored its five goals because Paul Kariya's ancestors came from Japan, Jarome Iginla's from Nigeria, and Joe Sakic's from the Balkans. Yet each and every one of them is a modern Canadian, and the national celebration that followed the gold medals brought together Canadians of every culture and community. This history is worth recalling, as our modern immigration law demands the recruitment of highly skilled people already fluent in one of the national languages. Think about how different Canada would be today, if a Canadian immigration officer of a bygone age had applied today's immigration standards. "So Mr. Gretzky, you're from some part of Russia, you scored at the bottom of the points system, you have no marketable skills, you don't speak English or French, why should we let you immigrate to Canada?"

Today's Canada is only one chapter in the history of a

young country. How will the next chapter be written? And will Canadians write it, or forces beyond our control write it, as our country strides into the global economy and a world made ever smaller by the communications revolution? Unless we have a clear understanding of how Canada came to be, of how the society we enjoy today took shape, we might not be in a position to decide what kind of country we want to leave to our grandchildren. Only 15 years ago, the Internet was a fledgling message-exchange service among academics and scientists. Even seven years ago, there was only a fraction of the Web pages that exist today.

What will be the "unimaginable" ten years hence? If we have a tangible sense of Canadian identity, if we know who we are and what we want to be, we can make better decisions as a society on how to cope with that unimaginable future. Rather than simply taking everything we have for granted and assuming it's going to stay that way, we must engage in a dialogue that goes beyond politics and government, to deal with governance – the art and craft of how we design and run our society. Whether we are dealing with changes to health care, the emergence of genetically modified foods, and the sharp shift in agriculture away from the family farm towards corporate plantations, we will continue to cultivate a sense of national identity and national purpose. We can steer Canada if we agree on our core Canadian values, as captured in the Canadian Charter of Rights and Freedoms, as a blueprint for constructing a marvellous civil society. This is the foundation of our future global leadership, and we have earned our credentials as a just and vigorous democracy, because the true Canadian miracle is that our country emerged a better nation from a brutally racist past. Ours is perhaps the first postmodern nation: one in which relatively open immigration and the largely benevolent application of knowledge and scientific discoveries have created a society that can draw from many strands of human experience.

A homogeneous population does not limit us, nor do embedded traditions stifle new thinking, particularly in the Canadian West, where the next Canada is taking shape from an astonishing cultural diversity in every one of its metro cities. In comparison to most other countries in the world, we are blessedly freer of sectarian strife, and the sort of insularity that leads largely similar populations (Ulster, for instance) to dwell on their differences to a debilitating degree. Most vitally, our national character was shaped in the earliest decades of our young history. The notion of celebrating cultural diversity may be a phenomenon of the last three decades in the realm of officialdom and legislation, yet from its very beginning Canada has been a country of immigrant dreams, indelibly shaped by the continuing tensions between its two largest immigrant communities, those of origins in Britain and France. Our unresolved national question has its ebbs and flows, yet it is the very vigour of our polity that enables us to proclaim confidently that we Canadians shall always find an accommodation. A country that cannot take its existence for granted will never yield to a sclerotic national life, and that is at least one reason to be grateful to the separatist presence in Quebec.

We will be a national space that is always being made. And we know as we present ourselves to the world, that the Canada of immigrant dreams will endure, no matter what form it takes at any particular time in its evolution. We do not merely exist, we flourish, and this is a message that is at the core of the Canadian identity we project to the world, and the Canadian values we seek to share with the world. That should not be seen as an arrogant imposition, but as an offer of what is best in us: it is part of the obligation that comes with our ranking atop the Human Development Index. Among all the statistics in the world, among all the ways of measuring a country's worth, this is the only one that looks at the quality and standard of civilisation nations have achieved. It starts with the traditional economic measures of income and output, supplementing and enriching that with a basket of social indices that reflect what a nation does with its wealth. In its essence, it is a measure of the quality of both economic development and social development, recognising that the two go hand in hand in the making of a clement future.

The post-war history of Canada has largely been based on projecting a certain set of values associated with that dynamic civilisation that comes from an immigrant society. It flows too from the sense of Canadian international citizenship that was reflected by Lester Pearson. The late Canadian prime minister won the Nobel Prize for Peace as the one who created the idea of United Nations peacekeeping, working with Ralph Bunche, Dag Hammarskjold and the UN Security Council to make UN peace keepers a permanent fixture of international relations.

~

We are the best country for three principal reasons:

The way we have accommodated and nourished the diversity of our origins;

Our efforts to transcend deferential democracy and its accompanying partisan politics, to build what might be called The Demotic Society;

The evolution of our culture of peace, emerging from a history of profound intolerance and the colonial subjugation of aboriginal communities and first-generation immigrants.

As these ideas take shape in the chapters to follow, it should be remembered they are animated by the truth in the immigrant heart, whether we arrived by choice, by chance or by force – the knowledge that come what may, this is the country where we will build our future.

So many of those who came here have lived and grown with this truth.

Barry, whose words touched his readers' imagination.

Nizar and Razia, whose refugee son 29 years later became Deputy Leader of Her Majesty's Loyal Opposition in the House of Commons.

Nella, who helps those overcome by their addictions.

Jan, who gave up computing science to sell wine, and built himself a Polish hunting lodge in the bush country of north-central Alberta.

The sum of that shared truth built modern Canada.

It is not difficult to find fellow Canadians who will readily point out flaws in our country. Yet for the last decade, this country has been "as good as it gets," and this is the Canada that is the outcome of our aspirations and our dreams.

As we Canadians strive not only to sustain what we have accomplished but also to do better, we have much to share with the world, including the central fact that we have incorporated nearly every facet of the human experience in our national melange. We have taken to heart the lessons we have learned from our own past, to build a culture of inclusion.

We have done so largely in the last three decades, without resorting to assimilation, with the least possible arrogance. Yet in that process, we have seldom assumed the burden of leadership – Lester

Pearson and Pierre Trudeau are flashes of brilliant endeavour in a generally grey history of self-effacement – nor the confidence to assert that we have something remarkable to offer the world. Indeed, apart from the determination of Pearson to find Canada a place among the world's leaders, and Trudeau's somewhat quixotic efforts to craft global nuclear disarmament, there have been few occasions in which Canada has proclaimed itself ready to lead. That reluctance may well be an outcome of our history. We are, after all, still a Dominion. Canada's evolution from colony to republic remains incomplete. This is not necessarily a weakness, because that larger sense of belonging to an Empire or indeed to a Commonwealth helped to shape our culture of accommodation. Nonetheless, the glacially slow pace of our decolonisation, from 1867 to the present, leaves us reluctant to believe that we are destined to lead, or even to acknowledge success let alone the importance of Canada to the world.

We can no longer be so timid and self-deprecating, especially in the world that emerged from the 11 September 2001 attacks on New York and Washington. The response of the United States reflected recognition that even in revenge and retaliation, it could not "go it alone". The US-led attack on the Taliban rule of Afghanistan was sanctioned by a unanimous vote of the United Nations Security Council – in stark contrast to the bombing of former Yugoslavia only three years earlier, when the US didn't even bother putting the matter to a Security Council vote. Moreover, the UN was given the mandate of establishing a transitional government in Afghanistan, and the US-led operation – abetted by Canadian troops, among others – continued under the aegis of not only the UN, but of the interim government established by the UN. This reliance on international norms and institutions, a welcome change after the go-it-alone US foreign policy of recent years, brought the further recognition that peace would have to be built and sustained – and that the world would have to pay for the reconstruction of Afghan civil society. Interim Afghan leader Hamid Karzai's success in winning pledges of billions of dollars in reconstruction money showed that far from an action to bomb a country into submission, this was in fact a liberation of a brutalized people from one of the cruellest dictatorships of recent years. One might have wished that the liberation of Afghanistan had been provoked by something other than a terrorist attack on the United States, yet the downfall of the Taliban gave Afghans the opportunity to rebuild a society shattered by foreign occupation, civil war and dictatorship. Indeed, the international intervention in Afghanistan shows that the strongest antidote to a culture of violence cannot be found in a mindlessly unilateral escalation of violence, nor in succumbing to the impulse for immediate revenge. Whatever measures were taken against a network of terror in the short term, there was an underlying assumption that the only genuine answer in the longer term is to offer the fruits and benefits of the civilisation we enjoy to the less fortunate of this world. This is the essence of a human security agenda. In that climate, the very idea of Canada becomes an essential beacon. That is why we have a paramount duty to address the inequities in our own society, to seriously engage the poverty afflicting so many of our children, to correct the social inequities that scar our civil society. If we can achieve the goal of enabling all of our citizens to make the most of their potential, by offering them true equality of opportunity, we will achieve an even worthier model of civilisation. Yet the task of correcting our own deficiencies should not deter us from recognising what we have.

In the aftermath of the September 2001 terror attacks, Canadians can no longer afford the luxury of reticence. *The Best Country* makes the case for Canadian global leadership – not from any sense of military superiority or economic might, but from the simple duty to share what is best in us with the larger human family. We must accept that Canada is indeed as good as it gets, and acknowledge at last that it is our obligation as Canadians to influence the making of a better future for the world.

TRUDEAU'S CHILDREN

PIERRE ELLIOTT TRUDEAU GREETED ME ON THE FIRST DAY of my Canadian life. There he was, rolled up in my father's hand, on the cover page of *Time* magazine on the 6th of April 1968.

I first heard him speak the year after my arrival, as he received an honorary degree from the University of Alberta. It was my first exposure to a truly global vision – the other honouree was the then-Secretary General of the United Nations, the Burmese diplomat U Thant. At the age of thirteen, I heard Trudeau's vision of what would come to be known as the Just Society – the Platonic ideal of a well-ordered state wherein civility, collective duty and mutual obligations held sway – and it began to shape my thinking about my own place in the world. Now, as I trace the evolution of my own ideas, I can say that Trudeau inspired in me the ability to perceive the similarities and connections in the world. His words and example steered me away from the sterile pursuit of defining peoples and cultures by their differences. His two great contributions to building Canada's civil society – the Bilingualism Act and the Multiculturalism Act – evolved into what would become Canada's *de facto* declaration of independence. The Canada Act of 1982, which brought the control of Canada's destiny out of Westminster's hands into our own, was the final foundation of modern Canada. The Charter of Rights and Freedoms in the Canada Act codified what many of us knew and felt by instinct. These three seminal acts enabled the evolution of what I would call The Demotic Society.

The word "Demotic" has the same root as the word "democratic," deriving from the Greek concept of demos, the people. I would not want to imply, though, that "Demotic" is used in this book to distinguish the vulgar from the aristocratic, as in the sense of the "demotic" Greek language (καθαρevουσα) devolving from "classical" Greek. Rather, my notion of "Demotic society" is an attempt to come to grips with the apparent disaffection of voters in some western democracies, their falling rates of participation in elections, the apparent disengagement from partisan and even elected politics, and the often-expressed cynical view that politicians are all the same. I am in essence crafting a term that I hope would become an addition to the lexicon of political science. I hope to make a persuasive argument, in the course of this chapter and the ones that follow, that a Demotic society is an evolution of democratic governance that can flourish in established democracies whose society is largely shaped by immigration. A Demotic society is a natural progression of what is broadly understood as western liberal democracy. It might be looked at as the next iteration of a well-educated, confident and prosperous democracy. In what ways is a Demotic society different from a Democratic one? The natural rivalry between distinctive political parties, and their competing ideas and visions, is at the heart of democratic discourse. At a certain point, a critical mass of people begin to accept certain shared principles, ideas and visions, creating thereby a broad consensus of the centre. I cannot imagine a country that perfectly fits this concept, yet there is compelling evidence of the emergence of this trans-partisan consensus in Canada.

Certainly, no one living in British Columbia could begin to accept the notion of a Demotic society as it applies to their particular polity, because partisanship is as raw and corrosive as it has always been in that province. Nonetheless, it is interesting to consider what has happened in the federal polity in Canada, and in the provincial one in Alberta. As the new millennium began, Prime Minister Jean Chrétien's Liberal government won a third term with its largest plurality in the autumn of 2000. The following spring, Premier Ralph Klein's government was re-elected for the third time, also with its largest majority. Both of these victories produced concerns about a "one-party state," or an "elected dictatorship" and the weakness of opposition parties was duly noted. More interestingly, the relationship between Alberta and Ottawa began to change from confrontation to a search for consensus and mutual accord. This relationship is one illustration of the emergence of a Demotic society.

The shifting relationship is in part dictated by circumstance – Alberta may be the fourth province in terms of population, but it is the nation's third largest economy. It is the most consistently reliable "have" province in Confederation, being a perennial contributor to equalisation payments these past three decades. An inclement combination of economic conditions and fiscal policy make Ontario and British Columbia fiscally erratic. Their ability to contribute to equalisation can no longer be taken for granted. As Alberta continues to lead the country in economic growth, effectively weathering fluctuating commodity cycles, it gains greater momentum and a stronger voice within the federation. Yet these are in a sense details. The catalyst for Alberta's rising influence comes from alchemy between leaders that no economic matrices can predict. In the months since the 2000 federal election, Prime Minister Chrétien and Premier Klein have crafted an effective working relationship, and displayed a warm personal regard. A cautionary note needs to be interjected – Alberta's strong economic performance was evident for many years, yet it took a personal relationship to make a positive and constructive national accommodation of Alberta's economic prowess. Similarly, an abrasive personal relationship between the prime minister and the premier's successors might equally easily change the balance from co-operation to confrontation.

Yet the relationship between Chrétien and Klein may equally entrench an attitude of co-operation, driven by Demotic instincts. The relationship may have existed previously, but it was subdued to the point of obscurity in the months that Premier Klein involved himself in the leadership succession of the Canadian Alliance. Once that involvement ended, the veils were removed. Premier Klein told a magazine columnist that – in different circumstances – he might happily have served in Prime Minister Chrétien's cabinet. The reasons for the mutual regard are fairly straightforward. Each is a populist third-term politician with an unassailable majority. Each is a centrist and a pragmatist, both starting out as Trudeau Liberals and evolving to the political centre as their careers and instincts developed. Each shares a breadth of experience in both governance and government. More subtly, each leader enjoys a personal commitment and involvement in Canada's aboriginal heritage, most readily seen in their immediate families. Moreover, each is blessed with that golden political currency, the "common touch." Each is always able to project himself in such a way as to mingle equally well with ordinary and extraordinary people anywhere in the world – as much at home with the servers in a restaurant as with the leaders of the Keidanren, the Japanese economic federation that includes all of that country's major transnational corporations.

Yet I would argue there is a more significant foundation for this extraordinary relationship. Each is a politician remarkably well suited to the current iteration of Canadian and Albertan democracy, one that is in essence a Demotic society. A Demotic society emerges when the adversarial drive of partisan politics outlives its usefulness. While that is certainly not true of all Canadian jurisdictions, it is most readily seen at the federal level in Canada, and in Alberta's provincial politics. Traditional political parties are in essence tribes – a form of collective belonging that emerged when democracy was too new, and it was thought that people needed something that would bind them, produce leaders in whom the citizenry would invest a great deal of authority. By experience, traditional political parties were an extension of the former power structure, whether in a post-colonial society or in a country entering democracy after a long period of authoritarian rule. Every country needs a period of traditional democratic politics, if only, as I would suggest, as a transitional phase to Demotic politics. The current experience in Indonesia, for instance, is the resumption of a democratic revolution long interrupted. The dozens of groupings that have emerged as political parties have perforce entered into coalitions of like interests – they are essentially negotiating the structures of governance on behalf of the groups they represent. Yet after a period, especially a long period of peace and stability, political engagement is no longer necessary to assure an orderly, stable and desirable life for most citizens. It is at that point in a country's evolution that largely comfortable sections of the electorate no longer engage in active politics – not even in the simple act of voting – because to them political engagement has little relevancy. This is seen in many circles as apathy, arising from a feeling of having lost real power and influence, and the general inability to change the attitudes of those who are chosen to assume political power.

The feeling of powerlessness, of disenchantment with a lack of real choice, is often advanced as an explanation for the falling participation rates in elections, and the evident disengagement of voters from the discourse of partisan political life. Yet I believe this phenomenon is indicative of a sea-change in the nature of governance – rather than evidence of a stagnant or even moribund Democracy, I would see it as an evolution towards Demotic politics. Rather than a clash of opposing ideas between readily distinguishable parties, the politics of a Demotic society is one of subtle evolutions of the status quo, of small ebbs and flows that result in larger social, economic and political changes in an interdependent world. Rather than a competition of strikingly different views, it is more an exchange of slightly different approaches to common problems. The grand scope of democratic discourse is diminished, and too often political conflict is a series of minor irritations and differences magnified into something larger. At one level this can be strength, because it points to a society that is by and large confident and well ordered. Yet to those bred in the cut-and-thrust of traditional party politics, a Demotic society can appear to be curiously passionless. A Demotic society will be seen by some as more of an exercise in pure pragmatism rather than old-fashioned partisan politics – unless, of course, it is animated by visionary leadership. Indeed, a possible consequence of Demotic governance is that governments, particularly those re-elected to third and even fourth terms, will lose all conviction. They will continue to respond to opinion polls, to "market research" that gauges every political advantage. In the worst case, the citizenry may see such governments as insensitive, arrogant and even corrupt – rather than as collectives so lacking in vision and leadership that they try to respond to every twist and turn in public opinion, as measured by their extensive reliance upon psephology. As Professor Andy Knight of the University of Alberta observes in analysing this Demotic theory, "Perhaps this phenomenon is linked directly to globalisation and the recognition by many that politicians are really not in a position to govern or control what matters to most people."

Demotic governance may be less preferable to the tastes of some than traditional partisan democracy – yet if its emergence is recognised and accepted, it can be shaped to build an enduring consensus that reflects the shared values and visions that shape our notion of Canada and Canadianism. Different political parties can still find a consensus, but the differences become more of interpretation and nuance rather than policy and substance. The prevalence of that broad centrist consensus defines the Demotic society.

The late Pierre Elliott Trudeau's celebrated description of Canadians as "radical moderates" captures the essence of this notion. In a Demotic society, the fundamental tribalism of partisan politics, the "us versus them" notions of political parties, become sublimated to the larger search for a voter-supported consensus on the issues, structures and scope of governance. Rather than the prescriptions of traditional democracy, whereby citizens invest enormous power in their leaders and expect them to govern according to a distinctive set of partisan principles, a Demotic society expects leaders to govern in accordance with the broader social and economic consensus that is by definition Demotic. The consensus may not always be well articulated – yet citizens will respond adversely if they perceive a party or a leadership is straying beyond the confines of that consensus. It must be acknowledged that the emergence of a Demotic society can produce confusion and (perhaps justified) concern in a nominally democratic state, as the partisan tradition diminishes.

These phenomena can also be seen as empirical proof of the evolution of a Demotic society in Canada. Alberta's Progressive Conservative government, for instance, constantly reinvents itself to capture the Demotic consensus of the time in the course of its three decades in power. The premier who slashed government spending in 1993-95 is the same one who increased spending by 24.6 per cent in his 2001-2002 Budget. That announced increase was later scaled back to the order of 15 per cent as capital projects were deferred in the face of tumbling resource revenues, and the bulk of the remaining increase went to health and education. Clearly, these are not actions of ideologically driven consistency, and it is difficult to believe any provincial government perceived as "right wing" would indulge in so large a "reinvestment" in central precepts of the civil society. Similarly, the Chrétien government's increased majority reflects the inability of the Canadian Alliance – which offered a strong set of partisan principles and policies – to tap into the broader national consensus. The Alliance actually lost seats in its Alberta stronghold in the last national election, and its repeated failure to break through in central and eastern Canada led to a stunning fall in its popularity amongst the Western Canadian electorate that had once thought of it as a vehicle to end Liberal domination of the national polity. And when it elected Stephen Harper as its leader in March 2002, it chose someone who had suggested the erection of a "firewall" to protect Alberta's riches from the predatory intent of neighbouring jurisdictions. This is hardly an animating national vision in a country where seven provinces depend on equalisation payments to bring them a similar standard of living and equality of access to Canada's opportunities.

This concept of the Demotic society, a nation of radical moderates, may offer a more useful perspective than the notion Canadians are in the grip of a one-party state. Indeed, the debates within parties, the differences of opinion inside the big tent as it were, come to shape democratic discourse more than debates between parties. In a Demotic Society, good capable governance is, more or less, taken for granted and the citizen can actually afford to disengage from the minutiae of governance, from the day-to-day events shaping our political life and get on with their own lives. Consensual, informed, and effective leadership helps too, as the example of Jean Chrétien and Ralph Klein readily attests.

This can in one sense be seen as apathy, but in another, it is a reflection of a society so broadly consensual that citizens feel no compelling need to be active in tribal or adversarial partisan discourse. It is rare in a Demotic society to find a true partisan, someone who has voted for only one party all of his or her life. Ask around your friends, your companions, your neighbours, your colleagues – their lives and their experiences are typically too diverse to be captured in a single narrowly defined partisan grouping. It is the broad political coalitions, the flexible ones, even the opportunistic ones who most effectively gauge public sentiment and opinion, who flourish in the Demotic age. Indeed, as the once-heady prospects of the Canadian Alliance descended into a farce in the Spring of 2002, the limits of ideological purity were clearly on display. The easy admixture of religion and politics, the attempts to inspire support by suggesting that success is only a matter of persuading a silent majority to buy into a partisan message, reflected an Official Opposition in search of a cogent identity. Even as the Alliance leadership unfolded, it was evident that simply defining that identity was no assurance that the party would be any more palatable to the Demotic consensus.

It is important to recognise the emergence of Demotic governance in Canada is a phenomenon shared with the United States, Britain and – to a lesser extent – France. These are polities that breed movements of broad consensus. President Bill Clinton's rightist Democrats, President George W. Bush's centrist (in an American rather than a Canadian or European sense) Republicans, rightist President Jacques Chirac's easy cohabitation with the leftist government of Prime Minister Lionel Jospin, and above all Prime Minister Tony Blair's New Labour bestriding the political centre in Britain are evidence of a political evolution. These phenomena rise above the old tribal divides of traditional party politics, creating new coalitions and networks of the centre. The Demotic evolution and the confidence it implies are an important element in the emergence of the borderless world, and the attendant possibilities of globalisation, once we transcend a fixed focus on economics alone to embrace a broader loftier vision.

As we have seen with Blair, a well-articulated sense of the nation's destiny injects passion into the pragmatism of Demotic politics. In Canada, that vision was for too long shaped in the Golden Triangle, the nexus of political and economic power rooted in Montreal, Toronto and Ottawa. The emergence of Alberta as an economic and political force, abetted in no small part by the friendship between Premier Klein and Prime Minister Chrétien, changes that traditional structure. It is perhaps more apt now to speak of Canada's national vision being shaped by a Golden Quadrangle. Alberta is now the fourth point, at last bringing to national governance the perspectives of Canada's New West – the only part of the country where the majority population is of neither French nor British descent. The image of a Quadrangle may finally enable "traditional" Canada to transcend its Anglo-French immigrant culture, and to embrace the energy of a new Canada crafted by the mingling of the world entire. Yet in an elemental sense, the very ability of Alberta to claim an emerging sense of leadership in the nation is the reflection of a Demotic society. It must be acknowledged that the Demotic consensus is a predominantly urban phenomenon – there is little importance or relevancy given to agriculture or rural concerns – most readily seen in the dozen or so Canadian city-states that are islands of concentrated population amid a vast geography.

And it must be said it is difficult to imagine a Demotic Society evolving in Canada without the leadership and influence of Pierre Elliott Trudeau. Indeed, *The Best Country: Why Canada Will Lead the Future* was conceived as Trudeau's cortege moved towards the door of Notre Dame in the autumn of 2000, and took shape in the fully Demotic national election that followed. As a dispiritingly pragmatic counterpoint to Trudeau's visionary life and times, we were mired in a campaign wherein mediocrity and cant masqueraded as virtue. Instead of a celebration of our country and its magnificent possibilities, the election campaign in the weeks following Trudeau's passing brought a ritual devaluation of all we have and are. It showed the weakness of Demotic society – without a clearly articulated *raison d'être*, without a stirring evocation of the possibilities of our national life, Demotic politics devolves to an exchange of irritations and accusations. Instead of dreams and competing visions, we were offered a particularly arid pragmatism, leavened only by the calculated malice of "leaders" too timid to evoke any meaningful sense of shared nationhood and the privilege of a Canadian citizenship.

Canada's November 2000 federal election brought sharp reminders of the limits of partisanship. Almost as a last gasp of invective in a country whose major urban centres were moving towards a

39

Demotic consensus, the anger and resentment of partisans gained free rein. Immigration Minister Elinor Caplan's incendiary charge that the Canadian Alliance is a haven for anti-Semites and racists was especially disturbing, because it implied that Canada itself is such a haven. To take the unsolicited support of a few racists for the luckless Stockwell Day's party, and to imply that most of the people in the party share those views, questioned the quality and calibre of the citizens who supported the Alliance.

Similarly, the charge from Tory leader Joe Clark's war-room that Prime Minister Jean Chrétien balanced the budget "on the backs of sick and dying" Canadians was an assault on the very nature of Canada. To make the simple calculation that health care cuts equal the federal surplus is one thing; yet it is an attack on the integrity of Canada and Canadian values to suggest that a Canadian government would deliberately let citizens die to improve the nation's finances. The Opposition Leader called the Prime Minister a "criminal" based on a highly coloured interpretation of Canada's criminal code, undermining the integrity of the country and the political system he aspired to lead. There were other accusations, but these were the most deplorable attempts to erode the dignity and worth of our country. When leaders speak so, their partisans are encouraged to speak in kind. It is perhaps no surprise then that the consensus represented by the Liberals gained so substantial a majority.

The more we come to grips with the emergence of a Demotic society, the better placed we will be to seek and demand the visionary leadership that can animate this great country and its citizens. We can do so with the confidence that the "basics" will be reasonably looked after, no matter which form of centrist consensus takes power. That should make us all the more confident then to pursue the possibilities of building an even better Canada, and offering an even more attractive model to those parts of the world where a culture of violence is far stronger than a culture of peace.

I would argue that we begin by recognising the scope and extent of our good fortune, if only to diminish the irritations, quell the anger and calm the rage, to explore the value of our country and its singular opportunity to become a model for the world. Patriotism has never been a fashionable commodity in our country; it is always a little embarrassing to our peculiarly self-effacing national character. Yet it is time for us to affirm what the United Nations Human Development Index confirmed in 1994, 1995, 1996, 1997, 1998, 1999 and 2000 – Canada enjoys the highest standard of civilisation in the world. In an imperfect world, our own imperfect creation is the best country. And with this standing come obligation of leadership that we are reluctant to even acknowledge, let alone embrace.

The notion of the Demotic society enables us to come closer to Trudeau's grand vision of "Canada deserves better." Not the Canada the campaigning partisans described, but the country we live in and love. It comes down to this: can we leave anger behind? Trudeau's life and example left us with a central question, arising from his denunciation of the arid passions of Quebec separatism and his disdain for a culture of dependency.

Trudeau's central question was this: Can we abandon resentment and embrace the greatness of our country? Do we dare to reach out with love to our fellow citizens in our own communities and in every part of the country, without in any way expecting that love will be returned?

I believe that question will be fully answered in the decades to come. As we build on the strengths of the Demotic Society, as we broaden our national consensus, we will become more confident about ourselves. If we can make that leap into unconditional love, accept our country for what it is, we will bring a new dynamism to the quest for growth and change. We will move forward for heartfelt reasons, with a genuine desire to construct a better civic space. The very experience of being Canadian should make us idealistic enough to dream of improving the country that is already the world's most civil society.

We can celebrate the gift of radical moderation (or moderate radicalism, if you like), if we move to the confidence and serenity our country ought to evoke in us, its citizens. That sort of confident and dignified leadership – represented in the past by people like Tommy Douglas, Robert Stanfield, Lester Pearson and Roy Romanow – contributed much to the creation of the Demotic society. In exploring the Demotic consensus, and examining the possibilities of governing Canada inclusively, I rediscover an idealism I once thought lost. My flowering belief that the Canada we should justly celebrate will become an even better country in the first decades of this new century is indeed the animating force of this book.

In an elemental sense, *The Best Country* is an attempt to revive and redefine the sense of Canada that seemed to follow Trudeau to his mausoleum. I am a Canadian because of Pierre Trudeau. He was an inspiration, even a role model, the grand architect of a country with two national languages that affirms and celebrates the diversity and richness conferred by the many national origins of its citizens. He was the only politician whose death evoked in me the deep physical sorrow one feels at the passing of someone of your blood. It was the mixture of intellectual and street-brawler, of philosopher and tyrant that made him a politician without peer. I still try to reconcile the man who destroyed the civil rights of thousands by imposing the War Measures Act in Quebec in 1970 with the man who brought home the Constitution. I remember the overwhelming pride I felt when the Canada Act and the Canadian Charter of Rights and Freedoms were proclaimed in 1982, making our country truly free.

Many of us who were working journalists struggled to maintain a professional detachment – his very energy, intellect, charisma and presence sucked you in and made you take sides. He sometimes evoked in us the last thing a journalist ought to offer a politician – admiration, even a grudging one. And dammit, I never thought his last exit would bring a surge of tears, leave me feeling so empty. He wasn't just another politician. He was an embodiment of everything my country means to me, the only politician who inspired me to imagine an even better Canada than the one we have achieved today.

Yet as I shared the deep emotions manifest in his final rites, I began to understand the challenges that can best be resolved through a creative consensus – poverty, inequity and the other challenges that cannot be encapsulated in a partisan political campaign. When I think of the possibilities Demotic governance brings, I turn to a day in Kingston towards the end of 1989, the day I broke faith with the Trudeau whose vision of Canada spoke to my soul.

I was invited to a gathering of civil servants, academics and thinkers, assembled to contemplate the Meech Lake constitutional accord. Before the conference began on a bitter December day, I walked the few blocks from the Queen's campus to Sir John A. Macdonald's house, the place where the dream that would become Canada was formed and nourished. I stood for a long time on that lakeshore, oblivious to the keen wind, contemplating this small, almost insignificant house whence Canada's first prime minister shaped a towering and audacious vision of a country that would stretch east and west, resisting in part the pull from the south. The dream would be made real by a ribbon of metal, a transcontinental railroad from the western sea to the eastern sea.

John A. Macdonald's dream was achieved by persuasion and guile, by all the art-of-the-possible wheeling and dealing needed to turn a lofty vision into a reality. No guile was needed to make Trudeau's dream come true. We simply had to believe in ourselves and in one another: trust our fellow Canadians to accord us the feelings of fellowship and respect that are the core of our shared values. Yet among the political classes of the day, it was too much to ask. Brian Mulroney let the genie out of the bottle by promising to recognize Quebec as a distinct society. That offer was a shelter for the insecure, a place of refuge for those who felt too unsure of themselves as individuals or as a collective to claim pride of place within a strong and united Canada.

The offer of special status was an affirmation for those who needed their fears reinforced; it was an easy deviance from the higher and harder path of nourishing one's very best hopes for the future of the country. I listened to all my fellow participants during the course of that day, and heard that Mulroney's plan was doomed. A deputy minister from Manitoba told us there was absolutely no way his government would support the pact.

I began to think of the consequences: what would happen if those who thrived on fear were told that the future would be even more uncertain? What would be the effect of rejection on those who were tentative enough to think that they needed the special protection of a "distinct society" to validate their identity as Quebecers and Canadians? I thought it would be a worthy challenge to explain that rejecting Mulroney was not a rejection of Quebecers. Yet that night, I changed my mind. It came after an intense and vigorous conversation with a senior official of the Alberta government. She agreed with every instinct I had about a Canada built on our strengths, a Canada invigorated by an appeal to the best in us. But she asked me to put more weight on the consequences of rejecting the Meech Lake accord. And she persuaded me that rejection would unnecessarily risk the break up of the country, as the fearful and the tentative would seek refuge in the false gods of separatism.

That was the moment I broke faith with Trudeau. In the practical world that dreamers need not inhabit, I saw a country not yet ready to be led by its best hopes and aspirations. This is what I put in my notebook on that windswept day:

> Many of the people there fought through the language wars: to them, the recognition of Quebec as a distinct society was the central importance of the Meech Lake accord. A rejection of Meech Lake would not just be a rejection of Quebec, we heard, but a rejection of the tolerance and understanding on which Canada prides itself.

When I think about my breach of faith with the prime minister whose Multiculturalism Act and Charter of Rights and Freedoms made it possible for me to become a Canadian, I find an insight into tolerance that I never gleaned from Pierre Trudeau. I understood in Kingston that dreams aren't enough: sometimes we have to respect the fear of others, the deep insecurity of others, we need to tolerate the hesitancy of the many Canadians who dare not dream on the scale of

Macdonald and Trudeau. And this is the danger of the Demotic society. We may in the end simply settle for what is possible rather than what is best, if consensus becomes an end in itself. The challenge perhaps is to find a better balance between the partisans peddling limited visions, and the timorous pragmatists who have allowed our dreams to wither in that fractious, hard-edged decade since constitutional reform died. If we are to pursue the fruits of Demotic governance, we cannot be so tied to the practical and the possible that we lose sight of the animating, driving spirit of Canada: the never-to-be-completed task of crafting a country that is better than the sum of us. Pierre Trudeau's life and work distilled the essence of that spirit. The belief that the best Canada is yet to be built is his legacy to me, and I won't break faith again. The Demotic society will work best if dreamers and pragmatists are thrown together in the same tent, working for common cause rather than partisan advantage.

If my own sense of Canadianism took so much sustenance from the country enabled by bilingualism, multiculturalism and the Charter of Rights and Freedoms, where did the inspiration for those three brilliant foundations emerge? It was no mere invention of Trudeau's, nor did it come out the blue. Rather, it was the fulfillment of a dream of Canada that took shape as the 20th century began only to be denied by the meanders of history. That first vision of what Canada could become came from another Francophone prime minister, Sir Wilfrid Laurier.

LAURIER'S CHILDREN

As THE CURTAIN FELL ON THE OLD MILLENNIUM, IT TURNED out that Wilfrid Laurier might have been right, after all. The Prime Minister who dominated the first decades of the century just past said that Canada would come to fill the 20th century, much as the United States dominated the 19th. There are all sorts of evidence to show he was wrong. We are neither the wealthiest, nor the most populous, nor the most powerful nation. Laurier's dream, which in the spirit of the day foresaw a Canada of more than 100 million people by century's end, was firmly planted in the unstoppable expansion of the British Empire.

While the vision of a large population settling a vast and empty land is nowhere near completion, Laurier's prophecy of Canada's place in the world may yet come true – if we dare to use measures beyond those of economics and demography. The ideas and ideals of Canadianism, the real and imagined country we have become, represent a powerful force. These ideas and ideals go beyond dry statistics. They are found in us, the people, and the kind of Demotic society have come to build. In a world of so much want and misery, the abiding strength of Canadianism is that our country is always a work in progress. The work was set in motion by Laurier and indeed by the politicians of his day. Their grand schemes to make this outpost of Empire the world's pre-eminent country may have been fuelled by a boundless optimism. Yet even as the course of history denied them their dream – the backlash against immigration, the First World War, the mechanisation of agriculture and the Great Depression all took their toll – we can now see the connective thread between Laurier's time and ours, in a new century of new possibilities.

The ideas and ideals expressed by Laurier and his peers all focussed on the kind of Canada they wished to build. They were not content to rest with what they had; they imagined what an ideal future would be. They set a destination for the country. Yet they knew as we know now that the building of Canada is never done. In our time, we know that so long as there are homeless people among us, so long as our historic commitments to Canada's First Nations lie unfulfilled, so long as there are children living in dire need, we know that our international ranking merely says we are the best of a bad lot. That's why I like to talk about the ideas and ideals, because the kind of Canada evoked in Laurier's time and in our time is a collection of individual visions and dreams, expressed in a country that today accommodates every human origin, and nearly all of the world's languages and cultures. This singular strength is what may yet make Laurier's dream come true, with a small twist. It is not so much that the future belongs to Canada, but that Canada belongs to the future.

Our momentous human experiment, the convergence of the world's constituent human origins within a single geographic and political boundary, will surely come to shape the world. The Canadian model of coexistence is the most persuasive antidote to the pervasive notion that strife and violence are an indelible part of human nature. When the bloodiest century in history offers its own deadly evidence that thirsting for war can be more alluring than questing for peace, the very existence of Canada shows that there is another way, a more civil way, a more harmonious way of living together. This model is no accident, nor is it an imposition. It really begins with Laurier's dream, of bringing the world to fill the vastness of an overwhelming land. It was the naysayers of the day – those who railed against immigration, those who interned Ukrainian Canadians during the First World War, those who excluded Asians from entering Canada – who resisted the accomplishment of Laurier's dreams.

In fundamental ways, today's Canadian model remains an ideal that is still taking shape – because it too is vigorously resisted by those who think modern Canada is an aberration. These are the government-is-evil brigades with their efficiency-at-all-costs mantras – people whose thinking is so warped by the gods of the free market that they have lost all allegiance to the common good. To them Canada is an affront to a Darwinian notion of the strongest flourishing in a self-reliant world that must perforce produce winners and losers. In this view, even human life has an economic worth: at some point, it is no longer efficient to invest money in it, so our system of public health care becomes just another commodity, an inefficient state monopoly. One forgives these people, and in the end one pities them, because they may never come to savour the greatness of the Canada we have built together. It is because of Canada and Canadianism that we were able to enter the 21st century with more hope than despair.

Let us remember how it started, with an often-misquoted sentiment that is coming true a century later than its creator foresaw.

> Canada has been modest in its history, although its
> history is heroic in many ways. But its history, in

my estimation, is only commencing. It is commencing in this century. The 19th century was the
century of the United States. I think we can claim
that it is Canada that shall fill the 20th century.

~Sir Wilfrid Laurier, to the first annual banquet
of the Canadian Club, in Ottawa, Jan. 18, 1904

That was the closest Laurier ever came to saying "the 20th century belongs to Canada," his most famous quote. But that's probably
what he meant. When the speech was reprinted in a book six years
later, the editor wrote: "On this occasion the Prime Minister asserted
the claim that 'the Twentieth Century belongs to Canada.' "

Whether or not he actually said those words, was Laurier right?
Did the 20th century belong to Canada? It has certainly been the
century in which Canada was made. The young nation of
Confederation – the Canada of 1867 would fit comfortably into the
Alberta of today – grew to fill the northern half of a great continental landmass. Our population increased sixfold, and as Canada grew
in size and confidence, it became a country in its own right. When
Canada's first francophone prime minister made his famous prediction, he was leading a young country to what he hoped would be a
brilliant future. A year later, Laurier would oversee the creation of
Alberta and Saskatchewan, open up the West to mass immigration
and usher in a century of enormous change. Looking back at Laurier's
time, from our perspective at century's end, the transformation of
Canada is nothing short of astonishing. And while the change may
not be so keenly felt in Quebec and Ontario, which were already well
settled then, it is most evident in the West.

What did Laurier really mean when he said Canada would fill the century? As is clear from his many speeches and statements at the time, he certainly did not mean a century of dominance and conquest. His measure was more profound: to fill a largely empty land with people, to build a modern country on the foundation of Empire. That vision did indeed come true, though not as smoothly or as grandly as Laurier might have hoped. The optimism of his day withered with the onset of the First World War, in which an entire generation of young men perished – young men who in times of peace might have provided the great surge of European immigration Laurier foresaw. Those who did come after the war soon confronted the Great Depression, the dust bowl of the dirty thirties. During the Second World War, the conscription crisis nearly tore Canada apart. And in the slaughter of Canadian forces trying to land at Dieppe in 1942 – a failed rehearsal for the Normandy landings that would begin the Allied victory two years later – Canada came of age through its enormous sacrifice.

Yet the history of the country, despite these setbacks, has very much to do with forming a nation that in many ways is a model for the world. "In the past Canada has been the pioneer in what I deem to be the civilisation of the world, which shall be based upon peace," Laurier told the newly formed Canadian Club. "The British Empire means peace and harmony amongst all the races which are subject to its rule." Justice and the rule of law would build a great nation, he predicted. "Whenever people live under good laws, well administered, and they are prosperous, they never resort to revolution." Even though racism was a fundamental characteristic of Canada's immigration policy in the first half of the century, Laurier's prediction has come true in the second half.

Canadians of all national, ethnic and racial origins have built a dynamic society based on the rule of law – indeed, the extent and scope of cultural mingling in Canada at century's end is rare in today's world, where only a handful of countries encourage immigration. Laurier captured and conveyed the optimism of a young nation that was discovering its identity, testing the limits of status as a dominion within the British Empire. In a characteristic display of ambiguity that has been reflected in national politics throughout this century, Laurier said, "We have found that our Canadian independence is quite compatible with our dependency as a colony."

In replying to Laurier's speech, Opposition Leader R.L. Borden was even more optimistic about the future. "Looking dimly, it may be, through the mists I can even now discern the future greatness which I am sure will place this Canada of ours not only in the forefront of the nations of the Empire, but in the forefront of the nations of the world." Canada certainly isn't the world's most powerful nation, or its most influential – and throughout the century we have been over-shadowed by the infinitely larger and stronger United States. But by the measure Laurier, Borden and others expressed – at that fateful first meeting of the Canadian Club, the toast to Canada was proposed by W.L. Mackenzie King, who was to become Canada's longest-serving prime minister – perhaps they have been proven right. Their measure of greatness arose out of a sense of peace, order and good government – and of creating an advanced and harmonious civilisation.

Certainly, that vision is reflected in the United Nations Human Development Index. As we have seen, the index does not focus on economic output or military prowess or any other such measure of what makes a nation "great." Rather, it looks at the quality of civil society – at the standard of living of the majority, and the quality of life. Those are also the measures the Canadian leaders evoked at the beginning of the century. Yet there was also an expectation that Canada would grow to match the US in size and influence. John Carling, a member of the first Parliament of Canada in 1867, wrote in 1909: "Personally, I join with those who predict that the 20th century is to be Canada's just as the 19th was the United States' Canada has this important advantage that whereas in the United States settlement went in advance of the railway, in Canada it is the railway that is the pioneer. Surely, with such an advantage it is not too much to predict that the opening of the next century will find Canada at least equal in population as in every other respect to what the United States is today."

That didn't quite happen. The US had 80 million people in 1903, compared with six million in Canada. Today, Canada has grown more than fivefold – to 31.3 million people, but the US has more than trebled its population to more than 286 million. Yet Carling's optimism didn't seem misplaced at the time. At a meeting of provincial premiers in Ottawa in October 1906, Manitoba Premier R.P. Roblin said his province could comfortably accommodate 25 million people. It has about one million today. Richard McBride, premier of British Columbia, was even more optimistic. "Premier Roblin has told you that Manitoba can accommodate 25 million people. It would be a pleasant thing for us to find homes for 50 million or 75 million people. British Columbia will not be a whit behind the other provinces in the great and noble work of building up Canada."

McBride was a bit off. British Columbia was home to a little more than four million people as the new millennium began. That sense of provincial rivalry – each outdoing the other to build up a huge population – was shared by Alberta's new premier, A.C. Rutherford. He saw education as the great building block. "I believe that in Alberta the universal education of our people is the greatest glory of our province," Rutherford said. "We have organised 140 new school districts in Alberta. And in the building up of our educational system we have taken the good features of those of the older provinces, having succeeded in taking out of there the cream of the teaching staff of Ontario. I am proud to say that we pay our teachers in Alberta a higher average salary than is paid in any other province."

With people migrating to Alberta from many different origins, education would become the great leveller, Rutherford said. "The common schools, I believe, are the greatest factors in existence for assimilating a mixed population and we will endeavour to make our system of education as good as possible." If the leaders of Laurier's time could see to the end of the century that began with such optimism, they would find much that is different from their attitudes and assumptions.

Their time, for instance, paid no heed to women's rights as the Canada of the 1900s was supremely male-dominated. Women not only lacked the right to vote, but they could not aspire to any public or overt role in national life. The vision of that time took little or no account of aboriginal Canadians and their rights. The measure of progress was population and development – filling what the leaders considered an empty land with the surplus population of Europe. There was a natural assumption that English-heritage Canadians were superior to all others, that it was their task to "civilise" and "educate" lower races and cultures.

A fully bilingual French-Canadian like Laurier was a rarity at a time when a great majority of Quebec's francophones, then as now, spoke only French. At that time, there seemed to be a reason to believe Canadians of French and British descent would make peace for good, finding a way to move forward together. Laurier was the first French Canadian to become Prime Minister. And the Quebec premier of the time sang the praises of federalism: "We have, it is true, many creeds and many nationalities in Canada, but we have only one country," Sir Lomer Gouin said in 1906. Today, of course, the French-English tension continues to hang over Canada's future, with Quebec's current premier planning another referendum on Quebec's sovereignty sometime during the Parti Quebecois' tenure in government, to happen on that elusive day when "winning conditions" obtain.

Yet Laurier would also find that many things haven't changed. The dominant political issues of his day still dominate the dominant ones of today's: trade policies, immigration, youth crime, the balance of power between governments and jurisdictions. Free trade, then as now, has been a subject of controversy. Laurier was convinced of the need for continental free trade, but he never pulled it off, because it was seen as Canada turning its back on the Empire to embrace the US On the other side were people who wanted a preferential tariff with Britain and the Commonwealth – a market of 400 million people as opposed to 80 million in the United States.

There was a suspicion about the US, that drawing closer to it would erase the Canadian character, bring in republican and anti-imperial sentiment. Most of all, it was a fear of dominance, that US immigration would lead to annexation.

Laurier's was the time of virtually open immigration, necessary to fill the land. The motivation was straightforward. Britain, the mother country, needed to import food to sustain its large population, and by the estimates of the time, Canada had 350 million acres of land that could grow wheat. Laurier's immigration minister Clifford Sifton drove the grand vision of filling up the vastness of the West. He made robust use of the 1872 Dominion Lands Act, which granted a quarter of a square mile of free land (160 acres / 64.7 hectares) to any settler aged at least 21 who paid a ten-dollar registration fee, lived on his land for three years, cultivated 30 acres (12.1 hectares), and built a permanent residence. The dilemma was there weren't enough British settlers to open up the land. Nonetheless, opposition to this grand vision of immigration was most vigorous among those who had settled earlier, primary from the British Isles. As Canada's Department of Citizenship and Immigration notes in its history *Forging the Legacy*, "James Wilks, a vice-president of the Trades and Labour Congress . . . wrote to Prime Minister Wilfrid Laurier (in 1900) about the impact that an influx of Scandinavians and Finns from Minnesota had on the Canadian labour market. Wilks beseeched the Laurier government to enforce the Alien Labour Act, a piece of legislation designed to prevent the importation of contract labour. Only rigorous enforcement of this law, claimed Wilks, would prevent Canada from being inundated with "ignorant, unfortunate . . . non-English-speaking aliens" who would do irreparable damage to the community. There was also widespread opposition to western pioneers from central and southeastern Europe. Excellent farmers they might have been, but in the eyes of many westerners this did not qualify them as desirable settlers. Only those who assimilated readily into the dominant Anglo-Saxon society were welcome."

Forging the Legacy continues: "On the Prairies, suspicion and hatred of this kind were focused mainly on the Ukrainians and the Doukhobors. In Winnipeg, the gateway to the West, the Ukrainians consistently equaled or outnumbered the combined totals of American and British arrivals between 1897 and 1899. It did not matter that less than half of the total number of immigrants to

Canada in most years (and usually far less than half) were other than British in origin. What did matter was what was happening in Winnipeg. And from this vantage point, concerned westerners saw sizeable pockets of inassimilable ethnic groups sprouting across the West. The result was a heated debate about "Canadianisation" and a cry for the government to be more selective about the types of immigrants that it let into the country. After Sifton left office in 1905, his successor, Frank Oliver, would heed this cry and chart a new course."

Yet there was no quick end to non-British immigration, even as Canada's leaders considered whether "lesser races" should be permitted to come. In 1909, for instance, it was possible for Lord Northcliffe – proprietor of the *Times* and the *Daily Mail* of London and the propaganda wizard credited with impelling the British Empire to victory in the First World War – to warn Canada against accepting mass immigration from non-British Europe. Leave that to the Americans, he said. He did not see "any reason why a purely northern people like the Canadians should allow their children to become more and more like the products of South-Eastern Europe. Do we not want on this continent the British ideal, which, with all its slowness is a very high one, dominant, rather than an ideal which has been marked by an immense immigration of inferior races?"

Plans to settle Canada with immigrants of British Isles stock, including immigrants from the United States, did not always match the dreams of those who opposed the "lesser races." Indeed, as *Forging the Legacy* observes, "Estimates indicate that between 1901 and 1914, over 750,000 immigrants entered Canada from the United States. While many were returning Canadians, about one-third were newcomers of European extraction – Germans, Hungarians, Norwegians, Swedes, and Icelanders – who had originally settled in the American West."

So Laurier's vision survived, even though it was only in fits and starts. The Canadian impulses of welcoming the world, which led to the admission of Doukhobors, Mennonites and Asians from China, Japan and India, co-existed with an atmosphere of resentment, more fully explored in the next chapter. The First World War, with the internment of "aliens" from greater Germany and the Austro-Hungarian Empire, led to a hardening of attitudes. As *Forging the Legacy* notes, "In June 1919, the federal government, reflecting the prevailing anti-foreign sentiment and influenced by the economic realities of the day, used the revised *Immigration Act* to bar entry to specified classes of immigrants. Among those to be denied entry to Canada were Doukhobors, Mennonites, and Hutterites, as well as all persons who then were, or during the war had been, enemy aliens. In 1918, groups of Hutterites, driven north from the United States by anti-foreign sentiment, had established ten colonies in the Calgary and Lethbridge areas of Alberta and six in Manitoba west of Winnipeg. More hoped to follow, but in 1919 they, along with members of the other pacifist sects, were barred from settling in Canada. They continued to be unwelcome until June 1922, when the regulation was rescinded by the newly elected Liberal government of Mackenzie King."

~

Deciding the future course of immigration policy brought tensions. Not just worries that Americans and non-British Europeans would somehow dilute the British ideal, but fear that non-white immigration would bring fundamental harm to Canada. The rising flow of people from India to Canada brought particular resentment on the West Coast. Yet the strongest advocates of Indian immigration were the ruling elite of the British Empire, who had such a firm belief in the natural superiority of British-origin people that they saw nothing to fear. The question was addressed directly by a great Indo-Anglian writer who would go on to win the Nobel Prize for literature. He was introduced – without irony – as "author and imperialist" when he came to lunch at a House of Commons committee room on Oct. 21, 1907, and said Canada should not be filled by the "white race" alone. "I do not understand how the Dominion proposes to control the enormous Oriental trade, and, at the same time, hold herself aloof from the Asiatic influx which is the natural concomitant of that trade," said Rudyard Kipling.

Pleas for tolerance did not sway the Canadian leadership of the day – as the head tax on Asians and other restrictions were to prove – but it is interesting to note that the last century ended as it began, with efforts to make Canada a place where people of many different races and backgrounds can live together. This has been a continuing theme of what Laurier predicted would be Canada's century. And even though grandiose expectations of a huge population have not come true, the sense that the Canadian nation is waiting to be built – that Canada's best days lie ahead – is as strong today as it was in Laurier's time.

That sense of Canada as a nation that continues to change and evolve was caught in a 1909 speech commemorating the first Canadian parliament. Laurier's words carry a resonance and relevance today. "It must not be supposed, however, that the work was accomplished when Confederation was placed on the statute book. Everything had yet to be done. Everything had yet to be accomplished. The union was a union on paper. We had to make it a union in reality.

"I cannot hope – yes, I can hope – that the work is accomplished, but it remains to make it a union of hearts and we are striving towards that end with a fair measure of success."

As we know now, the "union of hearts" survived a turbulent history to produce the best country in the world. And now, to make Laurier's dream of the Canadian century come true, we Canadians can embark on a grand adventure to take our country and its values into the wider world, to create new benchmarks of civility and coexistence.

How far we succeed in making Laurier's union of hearts a grand Canadian offering to our fellow humans really depends on how we approach the challenge of globalisation and the phenomenon of the borderless world. The poet Pablo Neruda told the story of visiting a nitrate mine in northern Chile in the 1950s, where walkways of planks rose a few centimetres above a floor awash with toxic and corrosive fluids. It took eight strikes and the murders of more than a dozen strikers to get those planks – just so workers wouldn't have to immerse their feet all day long. Labour conditions in the Americas have improved in the decades since, but there is still a long way to go before anyone can say that conditions in a typical workplace south of the US border are comparable to Canadian working conditions. In the age of the global economy, labour rights and working conditions are of paramount importance. They are part of an emerging global culture of human rights that needs to be nurtured and protected by Canada, and those who would join us in this endeavour.

If we can take our culture of peace and help make it the foundation of a new civic culture in the strife-torn reaches of the world, we shall indeed fulfil Laurier's dream of Canada as a leader in the world. Yet to understand the possibilities of our shared future, we must look first at the history we left behind. For all that Canada's story is one of grand democratic yearning – from William Lyon Mackenzie's polemics against the Family Compact to Papineau's demand for an equitable society flung in the faces of Quebec's seigniorial class; there is a darker Canadian history. Our ability to acknowledge it, confront it, learn from it, has shaped our evolution as a nation. Indeed, today's Canada is something of a puzzle, because it would have been hard to predict, from the first four decades of the 20th century, that the country we know today would evolve. At the very least, a look backward will teach us humility, diminish any tendency to smugness. At best, it will show the world that as we aim to export the Canadian model of civil society, we are a prominent example of how a society once imbued with intolerance, strife and exclusion can become an inclusive society that brings together the talents and strengths of the world in a single national space. What we left behind in our past is the present reality for too many of the world's peoples – a culture of violence, conflict and exclusion. To truly value what Canada has come to mean, we need to understand what we once were.

WHAT WE LEFT BEHIND

P RIME M INISTER J EAN C HRÉTIEN BRISTLED WHEN
Malaysia's Prime Minister Mahathir Mohamad challenged our repu-
tation as a champion of human rights, telling Chrétien in 1998 to
address Canada's treatment of its First Nations before poking its nose
into other countries' human rights records. While Chrétien defended
himself by saying Canada recognizes its shortcomings and tries to
address them, the autocratic Mahathir – who jailed his charismatic
rival and deputy prime minister Anwar Ibrahim on trumped up
charges of buggery – obviously touched a nerve.

He used the criticism thrown at Canada by every nasty regime
that doesn't want its own record criticised. From China to apartheid-
era South Africa, despots have declared that Canada's own history of
human rights is flawed. In the 54th anniversary of the Universal
Declaration of Human Rights, Canada is widely regarded as a champion of human rights. Yet as Court of Canadian Citizenship judge
Gurcharan Singh Bhatia remarks, in looking to the past, "Anyone can
see that Canada used to be a racist country."

Canada has done much to rectify its past, to develop a vision of
the kind of country we want to leave for other generations, in which
Canadians of many origins can flourish together. But that doesn't

mean the past should be forgotten. Indeed, to affirm just how remarkable Trudeau's animating dream of Canada became, we should turn a clear eye to how our country was made, and the past from which it emerged. The real Canadian miracle isn't that wide-eyed idealists decided one day to "socially engineer" a great country. It lies in the fact that a country informed with racist practices gave birth to the country we enjoy today.

Canadians should know how their country was made, even if it takes someone like Malaysia's prickly leader to remind us. Mahathir's criticism evoked the oldest and deepest affront to human rights in Canada's history. In the 17th century, the first European settlers to Canada met, conquered and killed the Beothuk, aboriginal inhabitants of Newfoundland. After little more than a century of European contact, the Beothuk were gone. The last survivor died of TB in 1829: those who weren't killed in conflict succumbed to imported illnesses or hunger, driven away from the food sources that traditionally sustained them. The Beothuk decorated their bodies with ochre. The reddish earth-based pigment earned them the name "red Indian" from the European invaders, whose ignorance led them to believe they had found a passage to India. It wasn't as though there was much interaction, peaceful or otherwise, between the natives and the newcomers. The Beothuk met a technologically advanced invading force bent on conquest, lost their land and their lives. From that murderous arrival to the middle of our own century, Canada did all it could to impose European values and a particularly unforgiving interpretation of the Christian faith on Canada's First Nations. Residential schools, removing children from parents and traditional communities, confining aboriginals to reserves, are all part of a history that wounded and abused Canada's first inhabitants. Despite the many attempts since the late

1960s to make amends – beginning with the 1969 appointment of Chrétien as minister responsible for aboriginals – Canada's treatment of First Nations remains the most serious blot on Canada's human rights record. Still, the search for longer-term solutions is now more seriously entrenched than it has been in the past, Gordon Campbell's referendum notwithstanding. But it's not the only one.

Until well into this century, the settling of Canada – the most fundamental act of nation building – was fraught with prejudice, discrimination and intolerance. The first official concerns about bringing the "right" kind of Canadian to Canada began in the mid-19th century, after tens of thousands of the starving and destitute fled Ireland and its potato famine for Canada. By 1871, fully a quarter of Canada's population of 3.5 million consisted of first-generation Irish immigrants. They were Catholic, and they had little reason to profess love and loyalty for England and the British Crown. There were attempts to organise large-scale Scottish settlement, and immigration from other parts of Britain and the United States. Between 1870 and 1890, more than 1.3 million immigrants came to Canada – many from the United States and Britain, lured by the prospect of an open and unsettled country. Yet that immigration set the stage for what would be considered today as massive violations of human rights. It wasn't just light-skinned Europeans who came. In those two decades, Asian immigration began in earnest. Thousands of Indian Sikhs, Japanese and Chinese came to British Columbia. More than 16,000 Chinese labourers came to build the transcontinental railroad, drawing the most arduous and dangerous tasks.

At the beginning of this century, there were other great waves of migration from Central and Eastern Europe, settling the West as it was opened up by the transcontinental railroad. Between the beginning of the century and 1914, more than 2.2 million newcomers settled in Canada, but only half of them were of British origin.[3] Faced with this ocean of diversity, Canada's ruling elite took rigorous measures to ensure that Canada would remain a white, Christian (preferably Protestant) and largely English-speaking country. In 1908, Canada passed laws banning the further immigration of Sikhs travelling to Canada. The next year, the writer Rudyard Kipling came to the Sikhs' defence. As subjects of the king and citizens of the British Empire, he wrote in his *Letters of Travel*, they should be free to settle in any of the imperial domains. In 1914, the Japanese ship Komagata Maru arrived in Vancouver harbour with 376 Sikhs, who were denied entry to Canada.

Yet this was but a small foretaste of the policies of exclusion. There were riots in Vancouver against the Chinese in the late 19th century. To prevent the Chinese from coming to Canada, the government in 1885 imposed a head tax that few could afford. And in 1923, the government formally forbade Chinese immigration of any kind. Those already here were permitted to stay, but they could not bring their families. The measure wasn't repealed until 1947. The arrival of the Japanese in the 1880s and 1890s so alarmed Canada's government that it persuaded Japan to restrict migration. In 1907, Canada decreed only 400 Japanese males a year would be allowed to enter. In 1928, that was cut to 150 a year and was stopped completely in 1940. Restrictions weren't lifted until 1967. Asians weren't the only targets of discrimination. Newly arrived German and Ukrainian immigrants were rounded up by the thousands and held to internment camps during the First World War as enemy aliens. This is especially ironic in that the Ukrainians and Galicians who came to Canada to flee the inequity of the Austro-Hungarian Empire were rounded up for having been

Austrian subjects, and therefore suspect. This forced confinement was in keeping with the prevailing mentality of keeping Canada predominantly British. In 1915, the government drew up an official ranking of preferred immigrants. They were, in descending order: British, Americans, French, Belgians, Dutch, and Scandinavians. After the preferred sources, the following were tolerated: Italians, Slavs, and Greeks. Jews were not encouraged. Blacks had been in Canada since the 1750s – the first arrived as slaves – but new black immigration was virtually impossible. So was immigration from Asia. Even with the restrictions, prejudice flourished. The government did nothing to stand in the way of the Ku Klux Klan, which waged campaigns in Western Canada in the 1920s and 1930s to "purify" the country.

Indeed, in a socio-cultural climate that classified Europeans into desirable and "lesser races" and put Asians somewhat below, blacks were considered the least desirable of all. As the federal government's history of immigration, *Forging the Legacy* observes: "In its attempts to exclude black settlers, the Immigration Branch undoubtedly reflected public opinion in the West and elsewhere in Canada. Thousands of free black people had been among the Loyalists who had settled in Nova Scotia in 1783. Later, runaway slaves from the United States had obtained refuge in Canada. Nevertheless, white settlers insisted that the Prairies be kept white, and in 1910, when it appeared that their wishes might be disregarded, they drove home this point. On learning that anti-black sentiment in the newly created state of Oklahoma threatened to drive a large migration of black Americans north to the Edmonton area, the citizens of Alberta's capital mounted a strong protest against Negro immigration. This spurred the Edmonton Municipal Council to pass a resolution urging the federal government to "take all action necessary to prevent the expected influx of Negroes" and the city's Board of Trade to petition the federal government to "act immediately to prevent any black people from immigrating into Western Canada."

Jews became the target of attacks in the 1930s during the Great Depression, when Canadian fascists, particularly in Quebec, sided with their counterparts in Europe and made Jews scapegoats for the country's economic woes. In the 1920s and 1930s, the Orange Order fought for the dominance of Protestants. An overwhelmingly white group, ironically named the Native Sons of Canada, fought to keep Canada white and English. One of the worst official violations of human rights this century came after December 1941, when the Japanese imperial government attacked the United States. All Japanese in Canada were forced out of their homes and their livelihoods; had none of them were permitted along the Pacific Coast, where nearly all had lived and worked. They were confined in concentration camps in Ontario, Alberta and the BC Interior, much as the Ukrainians had been during the First World War. The Second World War internment of the Japanese wasn't just detention: their properties were seized and sold by the state, and there were attempts to deport the detained Japanese once the war ended. During the war, Jewish victims of the Nazi Holocaust were denied shelter in Canada. Refugee ships were turned away. Yet from this climate of intolerance, Canada emerged to become a country that celebrates its diversity and champions human rights.

The turning point came after the Second World War. Canadian law professor John Peters Humphrey became the principal author of a draft document that was later crafted by a United Nations conference into the Universal Declaration of Human Rights. Indeed, the values captured in the Universal Declaration – which its patron Eleanor Roosevelt called a *Magna Carta* for all humankind – served as a model for Canada's post-war development. South Asians and Chinese Canadians were given the vote in 1947, and Japanese Canadians were granted the right to vote in 1949. In 1960, the federal government finally gave First Nations the right to vote – in the country that once belonged to them. In 1967, the government formally ended the White Canada policy, opening the doors to large-scale Asian immigration, and, in 1989, made a formal repentance for the internment of Japanese Canadians.

To understand how far we have come from that past, come with me to a Court of Canadian Citizenship in Edmonton. Picture the hall, with fifty or sixty people from the rainbow of humanity waiting to be sworn in. The usher calls the court to order, and in comes the judge: stately in his flowing black robes decorated with the insignia of a member of the Order of Canada, his deep red turban a vivid contrast to his judicial habit. This is Judge Gurcharan Singh Bhatia, the first turbaned Sikh ever to hold the post. Whenever he welcomes the new citizens, he speaks with passion about our country, its history, its destiny, and its potential. Above all, he talks about what he calls the Canadian values that define us – the written ones in the Canadian Charter of Rights and Freedoms, and the unwritten ones that evolved in the magnificent cultural mingling that defines our country. To reflect on Gurcharan Bhatia's life and times is to understand the profound transformation from exclusion to inclusion, from suspicion to understanding, from a culture of violence to a culture of peace.

Once, after many years of speaking tangentially about his early life, he sat with me and talked about his defining experience. "We never found the bodies, never found anything."

In the comfort of his Edmonton home on a foggy November morning, Gurcharan Bhatia recalled the murder of his father, his

uncle, his aunt, his great-aunts, his great-uncles, and his cousins –
sixty-four members of the Bhatia clan, killed in the bloodshed that
flowed from the partition of the Indian subcontinent in 1947. He
turns to look through the patio doors; as he shifts, the filtered light
catches the Order of Canada pin on his lapel. "Our family was gone,
just like that. My grandparents, they were in their 80s then, walked
200 miles from Mirpur to Jammu, to reach safety."

From that, Bhatia emerged as more than a survivor. He began a
life journey that would make him an ardent champion of human
rights, a champion of the "universal values" of non-violence, compassion and peace.

He was inspired by the challenge of teaching every child in the
world about the meaning and significance of the declaration. When
the declaration was adopted in December 1948, it was the first charter of rights for all the people in the world. It was an attempt to build
a lasting peace from the ruins of the Second World War – a time when
experiences like Bhatia's were far more commonplace than they are
now. Bhatia was trying to find his father and other relatives "as the
universal declaration was born," hoping they survived the cross-border
raids and skirmishes that marked the first months of independence.
For Bhatia, it comes down to this: what can he do to ensure that other
families escape the grief that descended on his own life.

Even with the passage of half a century, it is not easy for Bhatia to
recall the events of that faraway summer. His father, Ishar Singh
Bhatia, was the superintendent of police in Mirpur, a market town of
40,000 on the border of Kashmir and Punjab. Sensing trouble from
the imminent partition of India, Ishar Singh moved his wife and four
children to the city of Jammu, far away from what would be the border with the new country of Pakistan. That was in July 1947. Ishar

Singh and his brother Jagjit Singh Bhatia, a customs officer, went back to their posts in Mirpur. "We never saw them again."

Half a million people were killed within the first weeks of Indian and Pakistani independence, as entire populations tried to move from one country to another. From what the family was able to reconstruct, Bhatia believes Ishar Singh was slain in the performance of his duty. Aged sixteen, Bhatia had to provide for his three siblings and his mother Kulwant Kaur. How did he feel, once the shock diminished? Angry? Vengeful?

No, says Bhatia. The path of vengeance wasn't open. "My mother was a great influence on me. She said violence was not the solution." A follower of Mahatma Gandhi, Kulwant persuaded her son that it was necessary to renounce violence. And to this day, Bhatia holds the teachings of Gandhi as the model for his life. Another shock absolutely confirmed Bhatia's commitment to non-violence. The summer his father was killed, violence between Hindus and Muslims swept through Jammu. Out for a walk, Bhatia saw a slain Muslim family in a roadside ditch. A little girl showed signs of life. Bhatia took her home; a mob showed up at the door demanding the girl. "We took her over the rooftops, through our neighbourhood, until we were able to place her safely with another Muslim family."

His father's death, and the mob at the door, led Bhatia to question: "What makes human beings who believe in religion want to take the lives of each other? I started thinking, do religion and culture, mixing religion with politics, unite humanity or divide humanity?"

Bhatia and the survivors of his family moved to the Indian capital Delhi. Bhatia trained as an accountant, went to Glasgow, Scotland, in 1955 to study business administration, and married Jiti in 1962. By that time he owned a travel agency, among other businesses. One of

71

his trips brought him to Canada: "Because I was from Kashmir, I liked the snow."

Out of a curiosity to see what life held next, he and Jiti immigrated, arriving in Winnipeg in 1964. His sister and brother-in-law had moved there months before. When Bhatia arrived, he was only the second turbaned Sikh in Winnipeg – his brother-in-law Tej Bhatia was the first. He landed his first job as an accountant by offering to work free for a month. In his spare time, he went around to Sunday schools and community groups to talk about his heritage, to address "the fear of the unknown that causes apprehension, fear and prejudice."

He flourished in Canada, moved into property development, and by 1979 built up a business that he sold to a firm called Abacus Cities. It was another turning point in his life. The deal was in stocks and cash; he was to receive one million dollars a year for twenty-five years. Just before the first payment was due, Abacus Cities went broke. Bhatia never got his money and his assets were gone. In 1980, he moved to Edmonton to start again. But the end of the Alberta boom took away the allure of development. Bhatia spent more and more time thinking about the questions that had arisen after his father's death. He opened a non-profit community paper called *The Canadian Link*, and used it to advance an idea dear to his heart: Canadian values, the set of beliefs and principles that bind this diverse country. In 1989, he was appointed to the first of two terms on the Canadian Human Rights Commission. His time as a commissioner convinced him that the Universal Declaration was not simply a legal document. "It was based on real values, shared values like non-violence," mutual respect, a sense of compassion, a sense of justice, all the elements of civil society.

Bhatia came to revere the work of John Humphrey, the Canadian who drafted the Universal Declaration. "I looked to him as a Messiah, because Humphrey offered a set of values that were made available to humanity at large."

In a world where borders matter less than they once did, in the intense mingling of populations and cultures, "there should be some fundamental values common to all human beings."

This is what the declaration offers, says Bhatia, and it defines his goal. "I want to see every country in the world teaching the Universal Declaration in schools."

That too is a Canadian task, because those universal values are also Canadian values.

We had our conversation about his life on the eve of a celebration of the 50th anniversary of the United Nations Universal Declaration of Human Rights, and reflected on how many of its values modern Canada has come to embrace. It was one of many conversations over the years about the meaning of Canada. Our talks began in the early 1980s, about the time the Canada Act and the Canadian Charter of Rights and Freedoms became a reality. We were both disturbed by the tendency of official multicultural policy to put people in ghettoes, to encourage a benign apartheid wherein cultures were separate and equal. We believed in preserving seminal identities rather than forcing their assimilation into some overarching national mythos, as was the experience south of the border. We were in a milieu where "multiculturalism" was defined as giving grants to ethnic and cultural associations to propagate and perpetuate their own traditions. We believed that this would ultimately lead to an abundance of solitudes, if there were no attempt to share across cultures, across ethnicity, across religion. The fundamentally hollow concept of "tolerance" only invited acceptance of something, it did not lead to sharing, discovery and ultimately celebration. We worried about the future of a cultural mosaic where every piece in the mosaic was separate and apart from the others. In the early 1980s, I wrote an article in *The Edmonton Journal*, titled "Multiculturalism: A Kindly Apartheid?" and was roundly condemned by readers. The subject was so emotional that I could not successfully communicate my intent – to ensure the participation of all those cultural solitudes in the crafting of our collective future. As Bhatia put it in our conversations, there is a point where "cultural retention becomes cultural detention."

Rather than attempting to change the definition of the phrase "multiculturalism" outright, we wanted to evoke the possibilities of the country we might have, if true cultural mingling enabled all Canadians to bring the best of their traditions to the task of shaping a society and a nation. We decided to think and write about the shared beliefs and principles that had contributed to the making of Canada, the underlying values and vision that animated our country. Two years before the Canada Act, in the summer of 1980, we developed together a newspaper called *Prairie Link*, later *Canadian Link*, on which Bhatia lost tens of thousands of dollars. Yet, it had an influence that made the expense worthwhile. Bhatia drew on his experience as a promoter to put the paper in the hands of every politician, every cabinet minister. Its editorials were the product of our shared thought, and the ideas I developed and wrote about in the *Canadian Link* were brought to a larger public through my journalism in Southam newspapers. The idea we pursued so single-mindedly was the notion of exploring shared values – finding what all the cultures had in common, and drawing from them a new meaning of what it is to be Canadian. We spoke of nonviolence, peace, accommodation, a commitment to fair play, justice and civil rights, and above all, a culture of respect. We used the phrase "Canadian values" *ad nauseam*, because it was Bhatia's goal – an objective I thought at first quite unattainable – to make the term "Canadian values" an everyday part of the nation's political discourse. He sent our editorials to every politician he knew, and to many he didn't know. In the *Canadian Link*, he ran cheesy photographs of federal cabinet ministers reading the previous issue. And in each publication, there was at least one editorial defining and advocating the benefits of building a country on what Bhatia called "the Canadian Values."

By the time of the Meech Lake Accord to include Quebec in the Constitution emerged in 1987, the phrase "Canadian values" was indeed in wide usage, and by the time of the Charlottetown Accord, there was an entire chapter devoted to defining and discussing "Canadian values."

And while we seldom dwelt on it at any great length, each of us was animated by the vision of Pierre Trudeau. It was an impolitic time to mention Trudeau's name in Alberta, in the wake of the National Energy Program. Yet it was the grander vision, the notion of a shared polity built by radical moderates that led our quest to define Canadian values and put them in public discourse. Today, the affirmation and acceptance that we ought to celebrate Canada's values have become a catalyst in enabling a national consensus on the kind of country we want – reflected in the evolution of our Demotic political structure where in most orders of government across Canada, the parties best representing that consensus seem to have a perpetual grip on power.

The value and worth of immigrant origins was really explored and reflected in Canadian society in the last forty years, and perhaps before that to a certain extent, but certainly not as much as it is now. When you look at what we have in common, what the Canadian values are, we can find that they are quite close to what might be called, at best, ideals or, at best, qualities on a global scale. In 1948, a Canadian, John Peters Humphrey, became the principle architect of the Universal Declaration of Human Rights. When you read the Universal Declaration today, it still appears to be a fresh and modern document. Humphrey never really took credit for what he did, but he said that he distilled the common experience of human kind into one forward-looking document that tried to create a common standard of peace, justice, and freedom for everyone. Humphrey grew up in a Canada in which cultural diversity was not given much of encouragement. In his home city of Montreal, Francophones had to speak English if they wanted a job that paid reasonably well. In Humphrey's time it absolutely was not on to be anything other than an Anglophone of the right British-derived class – or a Francophone of the right seigniorial class – in order to crash the top echelons of Canadian society. Yet despite that social milieu, he was able to create an extremely forward-looking sense of what the world could be.

Much of the Universal Declaration – not all of it, but much of it – was reflected in the Canadian Charter of Rights and Freedoms in 1982. So what were the impulses that drove Humphrey to come up with a vision of inclusion, of sharing, of the task of building a world together? If you go back in Canadian history, instinctively there has always been a sense of trying to find the strong animating idea of Canada, which is to build something different than exists south of the border. If we say that we are not Americans, what is it exactly that makes us Canadians, apart from anti-Americanism? The most manifest act of anti-Americanism was really the first Canadian act of nation building and the war of 1812 in the battle where General

Brock resisted the American invasion into the Niagara peninsula. That was the first time that Upper Canada and Lower Canada, what might broadly be called the Francophones and the Anglophones and the First Nations, came together and decided that they wanted a national space that would stretch east and west rather than north and south.

Even today, as the continentalist forces pull us north and south, there is still an east and west country – decentralised, diverse, and full of possibility. And I would argue that this is because it is a country based on certain shared values. Some of these are reflected in the Charter, values such as co-operation, coexistence (sometimes called tolerance, which I think is too mean and narrow a word to catch the hopes of Canadianism) and certainly a recognition that there is worth to be found in every one of the world's cultures, in every one of the world's traditions. The important thing is to take the worthiest elements of those cultures and not to bring the hateful ones, not to bring the violent ones, not to bring the exclusive ones, but really to take the best of what exists and from it to craft a country.

There is a fine tribute to the Canada that has evolved since the indelible shame of the Second World War internment of Canadians of Japanese ancestry in a conversation with Japan's ambassador to Canada in 1999. When I interviewed Katsuhisa Uchida, he astonished me by saying Canada's experience with cultural diversity is the most valuable commodity we can offer to the rest of the world. It is, he said, a model to follow as more and more people from different backgrounds look for a way to live without conflict, and Canadian values are a fine basis for that interaction.

"Japan's basic strengths, including its work ethic, education system and investment in research and development have not changed at all," says Uchida. "They will continue to be the basis upon which Japan pursues its prosperity in the new millennium." And as Japan tries to find a new way of doing things, it will be looking for examples to Canada, "because Canadian values are becoming international norms, your value system is setting an international cultural standard."

The concept of national identity in Japan is "in a sense too strong" and risks making the country too introverted, says Uchida. In a diverse world, where globalisation brings together people from many different cultural backgrounds and experiences, Japan needs to fully integrate itself into the global economy, and to be comfortable working with people from a variety of national and ethnic origins. "Your value standard in Canada is born from all these ethnic groups that are here, and from them Canada is finding new value systems, an international value system,"

When it comes to western countries, he says, there is a feeling that "perhaps Canada can show more sympathy to the Asian way of thinking," which he says is based on consensus, compromise and accommodation – rather than confrontation and winner-take-all. Uchida believes the values and structure of Canadian society make this country a useful partner for Japan on the world stage.

That is the essence of Canada. And that is our foremost claim to the title of *The Best Country*, and the vital obligation that title confers, to fulfil Trudeau's dream of becoming a brilliant prototype for the world. Perhaps we need to see more clearly what our country represents, and what it means to those who have come here to craft new lives in a new land.

WHAT WE SEE IN THE MIRROR

LET ME GIVE YOU AN IMPRESSIONISTIC ACCOUNT OF A country some of you may know. It is renowned for its cuisine. Its chefs have won the gold medal at three out of the last four Culinary Olympics. The hallmark of its modern cookery is a fidelity to the innate tastes and textures of ingredients; each spiced or presented to make a harmonious whole. There are sumptuous wines to match the inventive cooking – the finest are so prized that they fetch $300 a bottle in the top international retail market, and they have earned their fame in competitions from Bordeaux to Verona, London to Hong Kong.

Its writers are acclaimed the world over, translated into all the world's major tongues. The breathtaking style of its film-makers, its audacious presence in television, video and new media build on an artistic legacy already renowned for dance, classical music, painting and the plastic arts. It is one of the world's most sought after tourist destinations, entertaining more visitors than its entire population every year.

It is a clever country. The information superhighway runs strong and swift, travelled by an astonishingly learned workforce – most school-leavers continue with some form of post-secondary training, and its proportion of university or technical college graduates is the highest in the world. This cleverness is not squandered. It ranks with Singapore, Taiwan and Hong Kong as one of the five most competitive countries in the world, measured by the World Competitiveness Index.

It is able to offer its citizens an estimable standard of civilisation. It is one of the safest countries in the world, with a stable democracy that emerged from a chaotic past of war, rebellion and invasion. Its population is surprisingly cosmopolitan, particularly in its major cities, where it is possible to function in any major world language. It has a strong manufacturing base, and sells much of what it makes abroad.[4] It is committed to open markets and open trade, and to the maintenance of a compassionate state. It has superb transportation and communications links by world standards, superb universities, and a civility to everyday life that is one of its most engaging features. Its citizens have the confidence and skill to flourish in any country in the world, and are equally confident in welcoming the world to their country.

Its geography is varied enough to cater to every taste, from maritime to mountainous. There is ample opportunity to escape a robust metropolitan life for the less hurried pleasures of the countryside. Indeed, it is said of this country that the land indelibly shaped its citizens' lives, though more and more urban dwellers seem unaware of this once-intimate bond. There are places to find solitude, and places to find frenetic engagement. It is in many ways a model for the world, the epitome of a civil society built on a culture of peace. It is also a country abundant in resources, the world's largest exporter of wheat and sulphur and the second largest exporter of natural gas, and will become one of the world's top eight petroleum producers once its abundant offshore reserves are fully exploited. You will of course have recognised this country by now, and all you need to confirm your answer is a reminder that its third largest metropolis enjoys daily newspapers published in Cantonese and English. Among the people you meet the world over, would many remain indifferent at such a description? Yet how frequently do we describe Canada to outsiders as I did, or indeed to one another?

In a vital sense, we have to prove the value of our country to ourselves time and again, every time a group of Canadians in a particular part of the country questions why our country should exist. We do not merely exist, we flourish, and this is a message that must be at the core of the Canadian identity we project to the world, and the Canadian values we seek to export. We should reflect on why Canada's ranking as the top country in the United Nations Human Development Index is more than a feel-good achievement. Among all the statistics in the world, among all the ways of measuring a country's worth, this is the only one that looks at the quality and standard of civilisation nations have achieved. Devised by the economics Nobelist Professor Amartya Kumar Sen, the index was meant to replace traditional measures like national income. If you use the purchasing power parity model of economic output, for instance, Sen's native India has the fifth largest economy in the world. But on the human development index, it's among the bottom countries – its economic wealth has yet to reach the lives of the poor.

It is not a coincidence that when we speak of projecting Canadian values, we are also speaking of projecting universal values. Ours is not the prickly individualism of the United States, where the triumph of individualism over a sense of community is a cause for celebration. The "western values" we represent can find much closer cognates with the community- and collectivity-based values of many other countries, particularly the Asian ones that recoil from the cult of the individual, mistakenly labelling this aberration as "western values."

In the first half-century of the Universal Declaration of Human Rights, there was no international institution that had the power to prosecute leaders who attacked their own people. The Universal Declaration was only a resolution of the United Nations. It became a customary law of sympathetic nations rather than an internationally enforceable law, because it was unclear who might bring violators to justice. Satisfying though it may be to charge tyrants with crimes, is it really enough? The evolution from arbitrary practices to the rule of law will be incomplete if we do not think about what comes next, after a tyrant is removed from power.

In the past few years, there has been an emerging recognition that simply toppling a dictator doesn't solve the problem. It is necessary to build peace rather than keep peace, to create a civil society that will become an enduring protection against future tyranny. We have seen what happens, when civil society does not exist, where there is no democratic and law-based system to fill the vacuum left by a dictator's fall. In Cuba, tyranny gave way to tyranny. Fidel Castro was a hero to oppressed Cubans when his revolutionaries toppled Fulgencio Batista in 1959. Yet when Castro appealed to the United States for friendship and alliance, when he asked their help in building a popular democracy, he was spurned. So he took the offered hand of the Soviet Union, and turned what might have been a democratic state into a totalitarian one.

In the former Soviet Union, there was nothing to replace the Communist Party, once it imploded. Those able to think freely, to act freely, to analyse independently, had been killed or removed long ago.

Without free expression and independent thought – the indispensable ingredients of a civil society – how could a future be built? Mafia capitalism – the ultimate anarchy – quickly filled the void. Building a lasting peace to create a society based on mutual respect and dignity is a complex and arduous process. But it is one in which Canada can provide leadership, guidance and assistance.

We often take our own civil society for granted, yet it can serve as a model for the development of other nations. After the International Criminal Court, that's the next Canadian challenge: to answer the "what's next" once tyrants fall. All the places where violence and conflict reign today will one day see the fighting end. But what comes afterward? Part of the answer comes from the Archbishop Emeritus of Cape Town, Desmond Tutu, who spoke movingly in a 1998 speech in Edmonton about the possibilities of replacing anger with understanding and even love.

In the "post-conflict transition," the world can learn from South Africa, said Tutu. It can learn that it is necessary to confront the past, to acknowledge wrong and seek atonement, to find redemption and absolution in admitting to the evil that was done. South Africa could have chosen a different path – wreaking revenge, or bringing criminal charges against the architects of apartheid, or simply doing nothing. All of these paths would have condemned South Africa to repeat the past, they could not offer a solution, he said. The most damaging would be to pretend the past didn't exist, to let bygones be bygones. "We in South Africa said 'No' to amnesia," said Tutu. "Amnesia of this kind is victimizing the victim a second time around. When you want to destroy a people you start by destroying their memory." Yet through truth and reconciliation, the process of healing that Tutu led, peace can come to a country's soul.

If there is any country where those dreams of a reconciled populace can come true, it is Canada. Emerging from the cauldron of our racist past we acknowledge the challenge of building just societies, yet it is the quest for civility in our own country that enables us to seek a more civil world. Canada's former minister of justice, Anne McLellan, offers one of the most pointed summaries of the challenge.

She knows that the pressures of the global economy make it harder for Canada and other governments to close the gap between rich and poor in Canada, "we too face issues such as the growing disparity between rich and poor, child poverty, homelessness and the unacceptable living conditions of many aboriginal people on First Nations reserves," she said in opening the 50th anniversary celebration of the UDHR in Edmonton in August 1998. Canada welcomes criticism of its human rights record. "I believe it's good" that governments are coming under more scrutiny. "One of the great accomplishments of the international human rights movement" is that "it has held up the mirror to our actual, not our idealized, social and political lives."

Quoting the Austrian philosopher Karl Popper, she noted the ideal is not the impossible task of making heaven on Earth, but the practical goal of "making life a little less terrible and a little less unjust in each generation." McLellan admitted that governments are the world's biggest offenders when it comes to upholding rights: "The human rights movement has been about individuals seeking protection from the abuses of the state."

While Ottawa "has a responsibility to promote and uphold human rights," it needs scrutiny and criticism to succeed. Canada is trying its best, "but expecting governments to safeguard human rights, on their own, even in a democratic society as open and tolerant as ours, is insufficient."

On the 50th anniversary of the Universal Declaration, Canada presented a report to the United Nations committee on economic, social and cultural rights on poverty, homelessness and other rights violations. Canada is willing to accept international criticism and act on it, McLellan said. "No government wants to be hauled before an international tribunal for failing to live up to its international obligations. Yet, if human rights guarantees are to have any real meaning, alleged violations by a state must be reviewable by an international tribunal."

Countries, "including Canada, need to be open to such scrutiny and be prepared for potential criticism." McLellan noted that since agreeing to allow Canadians to complain directly to the United Nations Human Rights Committee, "we have had the dubious distinction of being much complained against.

"But if I may turn that criticism into a compliment, I think this is indicative of a healthy and active human rights culture in Canada."

She predicted there will be much greater awareness of human rights in years to come "because people's concept of human rights issues is evolving" to cover "issues that were not even conceived of" at the time of the Universal Declaration. "As recently as ten years ago, violence against women was considered by all but a few radical feminists to be a matter for criminal law, not human rights law."

Yet by 1993, at the World Conference on Human Rights, governments had made the elimination of violence against women "in public and private life" a central plank of human rights. When the Universal Declaration was drafted, she said, no one could have foreseen "the human rights implications of economic globalisation" or the issues raised by new reproductive technologies or "the extent to which communications technologies" might "threaten" individual privacy.

Poverty and social problems may not seem as compelling as war, terror and torture. Yet with the evolution of an international movement to promote human rights, these problems will take their place on the list of violations, along with gender issues, women's rights and the rights of the disabled. It's part of an effort to show that human rights are not some abstract concept – they can affect anyone. In the next century, rights might seem as important a foundation of society as democracy has been in the 20th century.

The real challenge, former Canadian Foreign Affairs Minister Lloyd Axworthy noted at the conference celebrating the 50th anniversary of the UDHR, is to "establish a human rights culture." Canada wants "like-minded countries" to "do a lot more on education on human rights, so that people don't see it as something abstract, something that's removed from them, but that it really affects them directly; because we are talking about human rights including women's rights, children's rights, and those are things that come very close to home," Axworthy said in his human rights conference speech he wants to prevent and control "child sex exploitation, propaganda, hate, the kind of things crypto-Nazis use; we are looking at what kind of jurisprudence or conventions might be established."

The question we need to ask is whether we have done enough to establish that human rights culture within our own borders. We have an enviable society. Things work. Honesty is far more prevalent than deception. We treat one another civilly, respect and accommodate our differences, speak freely and mix freely. But have you ever really stopped to think why you take all these things for granted, when there is such a lack of them in so many other parts of the world? That's what being a civil society means. Yet as McLellan notes, the scourge of poverty, the spreading inequity call into question our own commitment and ability to better our society. Being the best country means never stopping to rest on your laurels, to be always aware that we have an obligation to build something even better and more durable, so that we may make some sense of what freedom and civil society really mean, in a world transformed by the bombing of the World Trade Center.

And if we want to know why we should value it, cherish it, and indeed offer our fortune to others, consider the experiences of those who left a once-lovely world behind, and still live with the shattered tesserae of a vanished homeland. Consider the experience of those who once considered themselves Yugoslavs, those Canadians who watched Canada join the NATO bombing of Belgrade in the fall of 1999, the city that was once their home.

In their moments of reflection, Nena and Miki mourn a country that no longer exists. They remember it as a country that offered all that was good in life – a home that once was, and never will be again. It was called Yugoslavia – not the truncated ruin that carries the name today, but a beautiful land of cultural diversity, ardent friendships and some of the most progressive social policies in the world.

"That is the country still in my heart, that is the Yugoslavia I lived in," says Miki Andrejevic, who fled that once-upon-a-time land in 1990, as the appalling rule of Slobodan Milosevic gathered force. And even though he was driven out by Milosevic, Miki feels a deep sorrow as NATO's bombs fall on his native Kosovo, in Pristina, a city he knows all too well; on Belgrade, where his mother and many family members still live.

"When we phoned my mother the other night, we heard air raid sirens in the background," he told me as NATO planes, some with Canadian pilots, bombed former Yugoslavia in 1999. For Nena Jocic-

Andrejevic, who left a Canadian life in 1982 when she moved to Belgrade after marrying Miki, the disintegration of Yugoslavia is too much to bear. "No one says that nationality any more – Yugoslav. But that is what we were. We were Yugoslav."

Nena's parents were from Serbia and Slovenia; Miki's from Serbia and Croatia – part of "the multicultural society" they grew up in, under the rule of Josip Broz Tito, who died in 1980.

That was the time before people started calling themselves Croats, Slovenes, Montenegrins, Bosnians, Serbs, Macedonians – the time before the old hatreds were rekindled, and the Balkans reverted to its sad history of strife. "We lost one Yugoslavia," says Nena. And now, with the bombardment of what's left, "I'm afraid we're losing it again."

Nena and Miki condemn Milosevic's destructive policies – the stirred-up nationalism that aroused an equally bitter response in all the other Yugoslav republics, until the country itself was no more. But they also feel a deep unease at the NATO bombing campaign and, particularly, Canada's participation in it. They feel there ought to have been another, better way. "We are a multicultural, peace-loving, peace-keeping country," says Nena – and Canada's intervention should have honoured that reality. "This is my country now, and I love it," Miki says, "but I wish Canada had tried some other steps" before joining the NATO bombing. The alternative? "The United Nations is the way to go," says Miki. "This is a multicultural nation; we should have had a multicultural UN force go there."

Nena is sad that Milosevic wasn't stopped when there were earlier chances. "Two years ago, people were marching in the streets (of Belgrade) against Milosevic," she recalled as NATO bombs fell on power plants and hospitals in Belgrade. "Where was the West then? That was the golden opportunity to establish democracy."

She recalls watching the early years of Milosevic's efforts to revive memories of past wrongs. "I remember saying in 1987 that I think this man is going to get us into a civil war."

He did, and the loss haunts them still. "Tito's Yugoslavia, for my generation, was something fantastic; you cannot imagine that life," says Miki, adding that there were free education, free health care, enlightened labour laws and the right to own property, to buy and sell homes and businesses, as well as ready availability of foreign magazines and newspapers. When Nena – whose family emigrated to Canada in 1967 – went back to Belgrade after her marriage, the Tito era was already over. Yet even then, she enjoyed a rich and fulfilling life. Nena went to work as an executive assistant to the Thai ambassador while Miki served as general manager of the Belgrade Philharmonic Orchestra – moving beyond a career in law into arts administration. "We had a wonderful life, between the diplomatic community and the arts community," Nena says. Yet against it was a menacing atmosphere of rising nationalism in Serbia, Croatia and the neighbouring republics. There was a sense of anarchy in the Serb province of Kosovo, where corruption left many in poverty even as spectacular public buildings were raised. When Kosovar Serbs came to Belgrade, en masse, to complain about deteriorating conditions, they were quickly sent back. In 1987, Milosevic went to Kosovo to declare that no Serb would ever "be beaten again."

Nena and Miki watched Milosevic's rise with disbelief. He gained prominence at a time of economic catastrophe, with 3,000-per-cent inflation. In the Soviet Union they had *perestroika*, "in Belgrade we had *catastroika*," says Miki. Even then, Nena was unwilling to leave. But Miki decided in 1989 they had to flee, after a deeply unsettling incident: at a family dinner, a relative "asked me to declare my nationality. I said I am Yugoslav. He said I couldn't waffle like that any more."

Miki was asked to declare himself a Serb, and he steadfastly refused – not the least in respect of his Croat mother, "the person I loved most."

Nena was quickly able to resume a Canadian life after returning here, working with immigrant women, and then tackling fund-raising projects for various institutions. The couple and their two daughters are settled into a comfortable middle-class life. They have tried not to dwell on the Yugoslavia that vanished – but when they see it going through another disaster, the pain can be too much to bear. Nonetheless, Miki is absolutely clear on his commitment to Canada. "This is the only country in the world where a guy can come over, speak no English, learn the language and become executive director of the Writers Guild of Alberta."

Not every story is so poignant. My father likes to tell the story of a tour he took many years ago at a stately building in London. "Are there any Canadians here?" the guide asked, halting before something of particular import to our country. Three hands went up. "Canadians," he repeated slowly, "are there any Ca-na-di-ans?" The three hands stayed up. The guide looked in exasperation at the three people with Chinese and Indian features, shook his head, and carried on with the tour.

"He thought we didn't understand English," recalls my dad. "He couldn't grasp that we three were the only Canadians there!"

For my anglophile father – London has been his favourite city since my parents were students there in the 1950s – the story of the confused guide is an endearing one. What could the poor fellow have known of modern Canada, after all? My dad's affection for England

– shared to a slightly lesser extent by his Francophile son – owes much to the memories of the time he and my mom were young and broke in a city that nonetheless offered them many intellectual riches and abiding friendships. Yet it also comes from another, more subtle impulse. Like many people who were born as colonial subjects in British India, my mom and dad never considered themselves inferior to the Britons who ruled the country of their birth.

This sense of self-knowledge enabled my parents to see the colonial period for what it was – a product of history and perhaps of destiny, no matter that some colonisers justified their plunder with the delusion that they were bringing a greater civilisation to a lesser people. I have sometimes wondered how history might have unfolded if my parents and their generation had in any way thought that Britons were their superiors, to be hated, feared, and above all emulated.

Which brings me to the bizarre tale of Michael Chessman, who had his fifteen minutes of fame in 1999 as he duped Canada's leading newspapers by "paying" for tens of thousands of dollars worth of advertising space with rubber cheques. When I began reading Chessman's very first ad promoting mandatory school uniforms and decorous female garb as the indispensable tools of social change that would create a "humanistic British Canada," I thought it was an engaging piece of satire worthy of Jonathan Swift, or at the very least John Cleese.

When no signs of humour emerged by the end, I charitably dismissed it as the pitiable nostalgia of some clotted guffin with a deranged longing for the Victorian age. I was wrong, of course. Chessman was born Mohammed Shivji – a name suggesting his ancestors were Ismaili Muslims originally from Western India. When a journalist colleague interviewed him, Chessman declared himself a white supremacist, and apparently hurled the worst invective at others who shared his ancestry, pigmentation and patrimony. Chessman – did he consider himself a pawn or a king? – appeared so ashamed of his origins that he erased his old identity and embraced a new one in which he pretended to be a Briton. He said he had learned the superiority of the British way of life while a student in Tanzania.

Of all the mingled identities I've encountered in Canada, this is the most bizarre. I do not want to speculate on the private demons that drive someone to submerge his identity in some mythic ideal, and to direct racial hatred at himself and others like him. Yet I wonder if there are less extreme examples than Chessman/Shivji – people who are fundamentally unsure of who they are, in the Canadian diversity. The answer to 'Who is a Canadian?' begins with citizenship, and many of the shared values that have evolved in this country. But we will never know the full answer, because our country is still being formed. We still have the freedom here to shape our civil society, to build the future as we see fit – a luxury unknown to parts of the world where long-established societies and their traditions hold sway. The definition of "Canadian" is enlarged with every new citizen who pledges allegiance to our country; as one of the few countries that still encourage immigration, there is an implicit desire to broaden and enrich the Canadian national identity as we continue to build a new and young nation.

In this grand project, the Chessman/Shivji dislocation, even in less extreme forms, is a pitiful reaction to an irrevocable change. Today, the London tour guide my dad encountered in the 1970s probably wouldn't miss a beat, if "foreign" hands claimed to be Canadian. About two decades later, I was checking into the Novotel at London's Heathrow Airport. When the francophone receptionist saw my Canadian passport, she smiled: "Which language may we serve you in, Monsieur?" she asked in French.

The signal difference between the old patterns of immigration and the new is the extent to which Canada's urban cultures mingle, the new definitions of "Canadian" that emerge when people of different backgrounds meet. It is difficult to imagine another society where the Knight family could have so easily set down roots. "I enjoy taking risks," Mitra Knight says with a smile, explaining why she left her native Iran at the age of seventeen for Ghana, unable to speak a word of English or any of the other local languages. It was the biggest possible challenge she could imagine, to break free of the numbing comfort of a middle-class life. "I just knew there was a Baha'i centre, but I didn't know anything else," she says of her arrival. "There were other Baha'is there, but they all spoke English."

So did many others in Ghana, a Commonwealth country in West Africa where English is a widely spoken language. But Mitra would not be deterred from her adventure. She spent the next seven years in West Africa working in social development – empowering women, helping children learn, and talking about the Baha'i faith. She quickly learned Twi and Ewe, two of the main local languages, as she worked in rural areas. English was another matter. "The only way I could stay in Ghana was on a student visa," so she enrolled in a data-processing program in the city of Kumasi, where the classes were taught in English. "I drew what was on the blackboard, then I would take it home and use a dictionary" to identify the English letters and words, and their meaning. "It took me forever just to go through one page."

Her experience there influenced her profoundly, she says. The people she met were "not involved with materialistic stuff" and were "really, really open" to new people and new ideas. What started out as an African adventure would eventually bring Mitra to Canada as a student and a stateless person – the persecution of Baha'is in Iran after the Islamic revolution made it impossible for her to return home. And it would ultimately lead the Iranian who fell in love with Africa to a Canadian life that took her from Halifax to Toronto to Lennoxville, Quebec and finally to Edmonton.

"I'm still amazed at some of the risks she took, travelling alone in West Africa, not knowing English," says her husband Andy, who joined the University of Alberta as a political science professor in the fall of 1998. His own life in the Caribbean island of Barbados was sedate by comparison. A clergyman's son who came to McMaster University in Hamilton to study fine arts and political science, Andy quickly fell in love with Canada and stayed. He has built an impressive career as an academic – an acknowledged expert on the United Nations and international relations, he brought the editorship of an acclaimed journal of global governance to the U of A. In an age where some Canadians complain about a brain drain to the US, the Knights typify the brain drain Canada has benefited from for years – the flow of talented, accomplished people from developing countries to ours. Mitra, who studied computing sciences at Dalhousie University in Halifax, can get around in a fistful of languages – she's probably one of a handful of people in the world who can speak Persian, Twi, Ewe and English; and muster enough conversation to survive in French, Arabic, Turkish and Swahili.

Andy's leading scholarship in international relations has brought him work as a consultant to the Canadian foreign ministry and won him prestigious fellowships and research awards. His fine arts degree isn't wasted either – several of his large paintings hang in the family home. Bayan and Nauzanin, their son and daughter, are good students who are fluently trilingual in English, French and Persian. The Knights say the diversity within their own family makes Canada an ideal place for them to settle – one of the few countries in the world where two people from Iran and Barbados could meet, marry, raise a family, and enjoy flourishing careers. Mitra found a job in the computing field at Grant MacEwan College. They like Edmonton, particularly "the international flavour" of the city and its population. The city is a comfortable fit because Mitra and Andy share a natural curiosity about the wider world. Andy wants to continue his academic work on "issues that affect the development of the world in the future."

Mitra would like to do more development work in West Africa. If she ever has the money, she would like to build a hospital in Ghana. When she left Iran, Mitra "knew I wanted to do more with my life." Her curiosity is a natural extension of her faith. Baha'is believe that all religions worship the same God. They believe in the oneness of humanity, the equality of women and men, and advocate world peace. Mitra says the Baha'i principles are based on "unity in diversity," which is also a good description of Canadian society.

Mitra took advantage of a scholarship from the World University Service of Canada, arriving in Halifax from Ghana in 1984. It was another complete change in environment, but she was happy to see some African faces at Dalhousie. On her first day, an Ethiopian student, Ambaya, offered to give her a campus orientation. As they walked around they bumped into one of Ambaya's friends Andy, who was finishing his master's degree in political science. "I saw his big, friendly smile," says Mitra. She insists that any account should say it was Andy who pursued her. "I've never gone after a guy in my life."

95

They married within the year, and moved to Toronto, where Andy pursued his PhD at York University. His thesis on global governance continued an interest that began in his childhood. Their home in Barbados was full of visitors of every background.

"Dad had people in our house from all over the world." Waldo Ramsey, a family friend who was Barbados' ambassador to the United Nations, particularly impressed Andy. "His enthusiasm was infectious." From his childhood, says Andy, "I had an interest in the world beyond Barbados. I had this notion that I would like to contribute in some way to the world."

If we want to appreciate why such an experience is important, why we need to accept our obligation of exporting Canadian values, we can turn to yet another of the many stories that illuminate the immigrant experience. Come to a middle-class home on a pleasant street, and enter with me the world within. There, Alla Tumanova's slender fingers wrap around a teacup of St. Petersburg porcelain – an imperial pattern in cobalt blue and gold – as her thoughts travel to that other time, that other life, half a century ago. Then, those same hands were wrapped around the handle of a shovel, striking the unyielding iron earth of a Russian Arctic winter in a prison camp. The sound of a piano wafts from the lower floor of her sunny Edmonton home – her husband Alexander Tumanov is giving a voice lesson to a singer – as she recalls a small, brief uprising against the soulless brutality of Josef Stalin's dictatorship at the turn of the half century: the uprising that brought her a 25-year-sentence in the gulag, the Soviet-era network of prison camps. "I have had many lives," she says, setting down the fragile cup. And of all them, the one in Edmonton has been most peaceful and fulfilling. Since 1982, the city has become a real home for Tumanov and Tumanova. They are among the 15,000 or so Edmontonians born in Eastern Europe. It has brought an abiding sense of freedom, given life to ideas like democracy and free expression, even a climate they enjoy.

A strong winter sun pours through the skylight into the living room of Tumanova's comfortable west-end home. She could not have imagined being here today when she was arrested in 1951 and charged with anti-Soviet activities. She was Alla Reyf then, just out of her teens, just out of the year-and-a-half of solitary confinement that followed her arrest in Moscow, a time that "was really hell, for me."

After solitary, she was sentenced to 25 years in labour camps. The three "boys" caught up in the movement were sentenced to death and executed – all for writing a manifesto demanding alternatives to Stalinist rule. It seems so far away now from her Canadian life: Alexander (Sasha) reviving his musical career after retiring as a professor of Russian literature from the University of Alberta; Alla enjoying a serenity she never found in her Soviet life; their son Vladimir a professor at the University of Western Ontario. "My youth time was extraordinary but at the same time ordinary," she recalls. The extraordinary part was the wakening of political consciousness. Alla served five years in the gulag – in 1956, three years after Stalin's death, she was given a new trial and released. She chokes back an emotion as she recalls her mother's face, all tears, during visits to the camps. "Even after all this time, I feel something when I speak about it."

Yet Alla places her suffering in a context: she wants to make it clear that she was not a random victim, but an actual opponent of Stalin. "When history asks, why did no one stand up to Stalin, I want to say, some of us did."

The movement she and the other teens organised was a call for a return to the roots of Communism – to the just and egalitarian society they felt was evoked in the rhetoric of Vladimir Lenin. Alla and her fifteen co-conspirators believed Stalin's dictatorship was a grotesque corruption of what they thought was the Leninist ideal. Her disenchantment began in 1948, when she was just seventeen – Stalin had launched a campaign against "cosmopolitanism" – directed against the intellectual elite, and particularly against Jews. "I remember talking to my aunt, telling her I had to fight injustice; she almost went white with shock."

Sasha, like Alla, was going through a disillusionment of his own. Born in the Kyiv region in Ukraine, he set on a career as a professional singer. Yet when he tried to enter the conservatory in Kharkiv, "I found out they would not admit Jews." The same experience befell him in Moscow, until he finally gained admission to a music school set up by a Jewish singer. "We were completely Russified," Sasha recalls of his family and Alla's. "We had no Jewish culture, and I am sorry to say we knew nothing of Jewish traditions. Our only feeling of being Jewish came from anti-Semitism."

As we speak, Alla and Sasha show a thick volume of one of the 20th century's great Russian poets, Osip Mandelstam. Haunted by disease and emotional breakdown when he died in a Stalinist labour camp in Siberia in the 1930s, Mandelstam left his family and friends with a memorable refrain:

> In Petersburg we will be together again
> Around the grave where we buried the sun.

Yet he left few written works – to consign them to print would be to invite instant persecution. The present volume, all of it, emerged from the one safe vault Mandelstam could find – the mind of his widow Nadezhda Mandelstam, who memorized every poem her husband created. When Alla published her memoirs, which I was privileged to edit, she took the title from Mandelstam's poignant farewell and called her book *Where We Buried the Sun*. One day, as we toasted the success of Alla's book with generous glasses of a little-known but delicious vodka we shall call "Tumanovskaya," I felt entirely humbled by the very fact that Alla had survived to tell such an eloquent tale.

By the time Alla and Sasha met in 1960, Alla had become a biochemist, her past known only to her family. Sasha was in a career that would make him a member of Moscow's famous Madrigal singers. "I had a few young men make romance with me," Alla recalls, but when she told them of what had happened to her, they panicked and fled. Sasha wept, she says. He adds: "The whole night, I could not sleep. I could not get rid of the image of Alla digging" the frozen ground. They married four months after they met, and spent many years living as "internal exiles" – they lived in the Soviet Union in body, not in spirit. They had a reasonable middle-class life, including a two-room apartment. But they never lost sight of the scale of Russian suffering, of the injustices of the past, of the injustice all around them. In 1974, at the first signs of detente between the United States and the USSR, Soviet authorities decided that ethnic minorities could leave, if they were invited to by relatives outside the Soviet Union. Armed with an invitation from a relative in Israel, Tumanov and Tumanova left for Vienna and went from there to Toronto. Tumanova was able to use her background as a biochemist to find work in a laboratory, after they arrived in Toronto in 1974. Unable to re-establish himself as professional singer, Tumanov retrained himself as an academic and became a professor – he finally got his PhD in

1985, aged 57, when he was already a faculty member at the U of A. Now, he is coming full circle. "My life is full of meaning again" as he founded and directed the first seasons of concerts by his choral group, the Cantalena Consort.

They will never forget the first momentous discovery that bound them to their new country. Visiting the University of Toronto library, they asked to see the Russian section. They were directed to the appropriate floor. "In Moscow, you would find the book you wanted in the catalogue, hand the title to the librarian, who would take it to a censor, who would decide whether you could have the book," recalls Tumanov. In Toronto, when they left the elevator, there was no one to meet them. After waiting for a while, they went through the middle of three doors – "three doors always means a disaster in Russian fairy tales" – and found they were free to roam the stacks. "We ran between the shelves like children, picking this book and that one, books we could never read at home," recalls Sasha. "We looked at each other and said today, today we have touched freedom!"

This is what Canada means not just to the Tumanovs, but to hundreds of thousands just like them who came together here, to shape the best country in the world.

How the Demotic Society
Took Shape in the West

"Do you know what separates China and India?" asks my friend Uriel, in the precisely modulated English spoken by graduates of New Delhi's elite private schools.

"The Himalayas," I venture.

"Actually, it's the Fraser River. Surrey is all-Punjabi. Richmond is all-Chinese."

It is the Summer of 2000, the last year of the millennium. We're sitting in territory reclaimed from Asia, as it were – the old Japanese-Canadian fishing village of Steveston, now a lovely Vancouver suburb just south of Richmond, where our friends finally decided to settle after spending many years of their lives in Edmonton. We've just returned from the Steveston float, where fishers sell their catch right off the decks – wild sockeye at $11 a kilo, ground salmon even cheaper – to a neighbourhood far enough from central Vancouver that $500,000 will buy you a comfortable home. We've had an exquisite taste of Vancouver's allure in the past days – a lazy afternoon on the Spanish Banks, shopping and iced coffee on Robson, a fine Thai meal at Montri's, an exceptional Czech-style Pilsner at a Granville Island microbrewery – all the pleasures of life one comes to expect in urban Canada. Now, we share as our friends' family light the Sabbath candles on a Friday night in the tradition of the Ben Israel, the Indian Jews who left the Holy Land between the times of the first and second temples.

Our friends' ancestors were shipwrecked off western India, came ashore and stayed – years before the big Jewish migration to India in 70 AD after the fall of the second temple. It is an entirely natural and unremarkable moment, the sort of thing that happens every day in tens of thousands of Canadian encounters. Just down the street from our friends' home, the finishing touches are being applied to a breathtaking Buddhist temple open to all, although it was built by Canadians of Chinese ancestry. This is the way cultural diversity works in Canada, although its success is rarely reported in mainstream journalism, which by its very nature concentrates on the failures – crime, conflict, clashes, and all the frictions of so many cultures meshing together under the name Canadian.

Like most of Canada's metropolitan cities, Vancouver is such a lively cultural mix that you listen to accents to separate the Canadians from the newcomers. Those who don't speak with the local accent are judged to be from somewhere else, although they are not necessarily foreigners – they might even be from another part of Canada. In Canada's metropolitan culture, ethnicity and pigmentation are no longer the definition of whether someone "belongs" or is a newcomer who has yet to be integrated. I suspect there is such a thing as a common culture in Canada's metropolitan cities – reflected in the way you dress, the way you carry yourself, the way you talk – that is resonant of what a peaceable world would look like, if every one of the world's great cities accommodated diversity in the Canadian manner.

If Canadian identity is composed of so many diversities and so many complexities, urban and regional, aboriginal and recent-immigrant, and all the constituent groups of that immigration, then perhaps the best way to contribute to the shaping of a Canadian identity is to identify what all those elements are. In a sense, the Canadian metropolitan cities are part of a global urban culture in which the standard brands of globalisation, from Macdonald's to Nike to Starbucks, offer a superficial homogeneity that defines the international urban landscape without necessarily touching the day-to-day interaction of people and their society. Where does this complex mix of metropolitan and regional cultures of astonishing cultural diversity and plurality take us?

To the recognition that in one part of Canada, the West, a new world is taking shape: one in which the best and worst of the borderless world mingle, in cities that from their very foundation were shaped by a meeting of cultures. This is where the new sense of being Canadian is taking shape. That collective identity, too long the province of people who insisted in dividing Canada into "two solitudes" of Anglophone and Francophone, is taking shape anew in what might be called the Third Solitude – the immigrant built Canada that is most keenly present in the four western provinces. The Third Solitude is a counterpoint to the notion of Canada as a nation of two solitudes, but it is also a robust expression of The Demotic Society. Unbound by long tradition, created perforce from a culture of settlement and mingling, the New West is the clearest expression of the evolution of a Demotic political structure. And one can only anticipate that as this Demotic evolution spreads from the West to more fully establish itself in the rest of Canada, our national character will be shaped by an even broader understanding of who we are and what we can achieve together.

If Gilles Vigneault had sung in English as well as French, we might have a new national anthem today with the same lyrics in both national languages. Western Canadians might have eagerly learned the French words, because Mon Pays/My Country could be as much about our part of Canada as it is about Quebec. The Canadian West, like Quebec, is shaped by its geography. The shared bond of prevailing against the forces of nature, only to know that nature always wins in the end, is a defining characteristic of both these parts of Canada. Vigneault's evocation of land as the soul of a people would find a strong resonance in the West, no matter that most of its people now live in cities, and that Alberta is the most urbanized province in Canada. Vigneault spoke directly, even if inadvertently, to the Western experience, when he sang:

> *Mon pays ce n'est pas un pays c'est l'hiver*
> *Mon jardin ce n'est pas un jardin c'est la plaine*
> *Mon chemin ce n'est pas un chemin c'est la neige*
> *Mon pays ce n'est pas un pays c'est l'hiver*

> *My country is not a country, it's Winter*
> *My garden is not a garden, it's the Plain*
> *My path is not a path, it's Snow*
> *My country is not a country, it's Winter*

And he might have been describing the collective memory of the immigrant settlement of the Canadian West, an act that took shape only over the last 110 years, as he continued his lyrical evocation of the land we share in "My Country."

> *Dans la blanche cérémonie*
> *Où la neige au vent se marie*

Dans ce pays de poudrerie
Mon père a fait bâtir maison
Et je m'en vais être fidèle
À sa manière à son modèle
La chambre d'amis sera telle
Qu'on viendra des autres saisons
Pour se bâtir à côté d'elle

In the white ceremony
Where snow marries wind
In this flurried land
My father built our home
To this I am faithful
To his way, to his example:
And space for our friends so ample,
They will come from other seasons
To build and build again[5]

It is one of the misfortunes of modern Canada that our regional identities should seem so mutually exclusive, when the experience of being Canadian is something so intrinsic to our blood and to our soul.

Yet within our own country, because of our geography, we often find ourselves unable to recognise one another, to the point that Gilles Vigneault's intimately Canadian evocation of land finds its primary resonance in Quebec.

Unfortunately, Quebec and the West speak different languages, and the poetry of one does not often resonate with the other, even though it describes similarities rather than difference. Yet the one common characteristic shared by many citizens in Quebec and the West is a sense of distance and disenchantment from the national government, no matter who forms it or who holds the reins of power. Indeed, Canada may be at the point when "what does the West want?" becomes as exasperated and enigmatic a question as "what does Quebec want?" was in the 1980s and 1990s. There are two streams of Western disaffection. One is born of confidence, the other of fear. The first is rooted in cosmopolitan urban cities, the latter in its smaller centres and rural communities. Yet both share the view that the country east of the Manitoba border is an older Canadian model, one with little relevance or resonance for people west of it. If the older Canada represents Two Solitudes, then the nine million people of the West are Canada's Third Solitude.

Professor Manoly Lupul, of the University of Alberta's Canadian Centre for Ukrainian Studies, was among the first to develop multiculturalism as an intellectual framework in the Canadian West. He understood that the description of the Two Solitudes did not describe the sensibilities of the West of the country. The West, from its very beginnings, was shaped by cultural diversity, its non-aboriginal population arriving directly from massive immigrant settlement over a relatively short period of time. Lupul, like Westerners of today, did not necessarily recognize himself in the standard evocation of the "duality" of the country, the one that makes "sense" east of the Manitoba border.

Indeed, the duality is more and more a historic reality rather than a current descriptor in the other metro cities that are as diverse as the Western ones. Montreal, Toronto and to a much lesser extent Ottawa are by now a melange of immigrant streams. Yet the difference between the West and East is this: even though people who aren't white are now a majority in the City of Toronto, its founding matrix is still the Anglo-Scottish heritage that has dominated the city for most of its existence. Similarly, the foundation of Montreal remains proudly francophone, rooted in the French-Irish-Catholic tradition that has been the city's sustaining ethos. Ottawa, with its uneasy dynamic between the better-off Anglos on the Ontario side and the poorer-cousin Francophones on the Quebec side, embodies the Old Canada's creative tension, and all the diversity of recent years is injected into that matrix. The metro cities of the West, by contrast, are authentic cities of migration and immigration, young and recent conurbations that more than anything else provide a civic space for cultural mingling, and in so doing become a template for progress and prosperity in a borderless world. It is in the four metro cities of the West that Canada is building its most vital model for the world, a resonant example of how people of diverse origins can indeed flourish under shared Canadian values, united by a Charter of Rights and Freedoms, and gain there from a resolute sense of citizenship.

We in the West are told Canada is a country of two "founding" nations. It's about people who came from the British Isles and people who came from France. Where does that leave our aboriginal people and the rest of us? The majority population of the West is of neither French nor British descent – indeed in Winnipeg, Vancouver, Calgary and Edmonton fewer than one in seven citizens are of pure "founding nations" heritage. Canada's largest urban centres are havens of cultural diversity; and the West is in fact the most ethnically diverse part of the country, especially in its metro cities.[6]

The West is home to what might realistically be called Canada's Third Solitude. We are the Other Canadians. We "non-founding nations" Canadians are 15 million strong across the country, but are the majority population only in the West. Yet in a fundamental quest to define the future of our country, we Other Canadians – we mongrel Canadians – who have always been the dominant demographic of the West – are largely outsiders. The prime ministers of the last thirty-eight years have been either British or French. We Other Canadians might get to see a Schreyer or a Hnatyshyn as governor-general; or a Klein, a Dosanjh and a Romanow as premier; or a Dhaliwal, a Chan and a Mazankowski as a federal cabinet minister. Yet we perceive that we are shut out from most of the national leadership roles that seem to be the Divine right of *pure laine* Francophones or dyed-in-the-wool Anglos. When the West mentions "founding nations," we tend to think firstly of Siksika, Cree, Haida, Dene, Peigan, Inuvialuit, Nisga'a. If there is a Western concept of a European involvement in "founding nations," it is the Metis of Canada. To the enlightened and cosmopolitan Westerner, everyone outside the First Nations and the Metis is an immigrant. We are proudly Canadian, but we know we are newcomers nonetheless.

The "redneck" stereotype may be easy shorthand for the West, but as the immigrant experience and cultural diversity illustrates, it is a facile description of the Western diversity. Some 140 of the 209 Edmonton Public Schools teach French from Kindergarten to Grade 12, and there are fourteen schools – including Western Canada's largest high school – that offer full French immersion programs. In addition, there are francophone schools in Edmonton in which only French is taught, and it is possible to study to a BA or BSc degree entirely in French through the University of Alberta's Faculte Saint-Jean. This is not an image of the West frequently seen in the redneck caricature. Most children in Edmonton's public school system will have been exposed to both national languages at some point in their schooling by the time they graduate. Further, Edmonton Public Schools have bilingual programs in Cree, Ukrainian, German, Arabic and Mandarin and offer classes in seventeen heritage languages in all.

Linguistic fluency leads perforce to cultural fluency, and this is a vivid reflection of the diversity of the Urban West. These language choices are voluntary, and there is a waiting list for most immersion programs. This is an elemental formation for success in the borderless world. While a small group decries official bilingualism, the cosmopolitan face of the immigrant-shaped West recognizes the value of knowing the two national languages, besides any heritage languages inherited from parents and grandparents.

It is important to remember the immigrant context, if only to understand that Western alienation or disaffection flows not so much from an opposition to a specific government, but to a perceived inadequacy in the structures of governance itself. This is borne out by recent history.

When Preston Manning launched the Reform Party in 1986 with the slogan "the West wants in," the West was already in. It was a dominant part of a majority Progressive Conservative government with a huge western power base, and front-bench cabinet ministers who shaped and influenced the governance of Canada. For the first time since John Diefenbaker, the West had a firm grip on the reins of national governance and influence. Yet even that exercise of significant federal political power was not enough to becalm the ardent heart of Western alienation. Offered the chance to lead on pan-Canadian terms, those bred in the culture of resentment spurned the leadership opportunity and ran back to the familiar and corrosive mythology of oppression. The Reform Party believed it should lead the country according to what it presumed were the priorities, values and interests of the Canadian West, particularly Alberta and British Columbia. The Reform Party did not see its agenda reflected in the real and substantial power enjoyed by the West in the Mulroney years. It is perhaps an understandable response, when one's founding illusions are shattered.

The Mulroney government came up with the Charlottetown accord to amend the constitution, giving the West something very close to the Elected, Effective and Equal Senate that was meant to address the fundamental western grievance about lack of power. The Charlottetown Accord had 2.5 of the three Es, offering an elected, effective and equitable Senate. It was roundly rejected, as the all-or-nothing sense of western resentment would brook no compromise. That rejection moved the Reform Party from an interesting concept to major political force. The face of Western alienation, captured in the Reform Party movement, had its roots in a deep-seated history that went back to the beginnings of the immigrant West. It was never the dominant history or even the majority's history – the Winnipeg general strike, the evolution of democratic socialism, the compassionate and egalitarian traditions represented in Prairie populism, the history of immigrant co-existence are all a counterpoint to the bitterness of the culture of the protest. Indeed, the success of earlier movements of Western populism, as seen to some extent in the Progressives and to a much greater extent in the Cooperative Commonwealth Federation, took a more generous view of the country and of its possibilities. Yet the anger inherent in the Reform movement was also a force in the evolution of the populist consciousness – across the years, a cocktail of resentments has fermented a harsh brew. Rather than embrace the "*beau risque*" of sharing in the governance of Canada, the alienation represented by Reform nurtured the old grievances:

The "eastern" banks that wouldn't give loans and watched prairie farms blow away in the 1930s;

The "East" acted as though it was the master and the west the slave; hung Louis Riel when he sought his rightful measure of power;

The "East" that had the temerity to claim natural resources belonged to all of Canada; and tried to take them away because the West wasn't strong enough to build a firewall;

The "East" that sent its Prime Minister Pierre Trudeau to ask why he should sell the western farmers' wheat.

All those winters of western discontent melded into one, until that old alienation became an anger that would not abate. As in Quebec, the western rage against Ottawa was in many ways a culture of resentment, very much the fury of the victim against an oppressor, of a newly liberated colony against the old colonial power. The showing of the east's "true colours," the National Energy Program that capped energy prices in the 1980s, blew away evidence contradicting this perception – like Canada paying higher-than-world prices for Alberta oil for the decades before the global energy crisis of the 1970s. Against this mythology, of course, is the reality of history. The reality of the Cooperative Commonwealth Federation (CCF) which believed in a strong central government and a Canada united by compassion and a celebration of its diversity. Indeed, the CCF governments in Saskatchewan offered a potent alternative to the sort of populism that bred a culture of resentment and disaffection. In its policies we see the roots of the Demotic society, of cultural mingling, of a Western province and population defining itself on its own terms rather than accepting (and resenting) definitions imposed by others. Sadly, the CCF's glory days were a distant memory when the Reform Party was in full cry, and the culture of resentment they nourished sank deeply into the psyche of the provinces west of Saskatchewan, the birthplace of the CCF.

Yet times have changed so significantly that culture of resentment no longer rings true. The disaffected of the urban West are the flag-bearers of a new era of lean government and low taxes, driving the "high-speed train" to the new frontiers of the global economy. The new face of alienation is born of confidence, not fear. It is not the face of the victim, but of the presumptive master, railing at an old order that will not fade or at least "get out of the way." There is more than a touch of American influence here, because this "get out of our way or we'll move South" shout is loudest in Calgary, the most American-influenced city in Canada. Calgary is a city whose overarching civic culture – one that newcomers seem to imbibe as readily as though it were a founding mythos – carries an inbred aversion to governance. This is in contrast to the "government as partner" ethos of Vancouver, Edmonton and Winnipeg.

Paradoxically, Calgary is the city where the robust agenda of Western excellence is strongly manifest, yet Calgary's leadership elite carries a strong element of the older rural alienation in its soul.

After 10 PM on a summer Saturday, there's a full crowd in the bar at Teatro, waiting for a dinner table in one of Calgary's most stylish restaurants. The converted ground floor of an old-fashioned bank with impossibly high ceilings and fluted columns, this downtown stage is a marriage of the showy and the substantial that represents the essence of Calgary's moneyed folk, and the many more who aspire to join the club. You're greeted at the door by a $400 floral arrangement and a $12-an-hour hostess in couturier black, offered a glass at the bar while they get a table ready. It's handled with genuine panache, as the crowd swells with people leaving the convention centre across the street, where Stockwell Day has just surged ahead of Preston Manning in the contest to lead the Canadian Reform Conservative

Alliance, the latest Western attempt to launch a political movement that will storm the bastions of national power and bring it home to Alberta. Day's solid lead is the talk of the bar, as crantinis and malt scotches pave the way to the crisp tables with their complement of aproned waiters. This is the new face of western alienation, far from the farmers who fear the government will confiscate their guns, and the folks who fret over the foreign farm subsidies that condemn them to a life of struggle and uncertainty.

You get everything at Teatro from pecan-crusted goat cheese to designer pizza, and wines to match. A Château Latour at $2,500 the bottle is the star attraction of the wine list, and there is a generous selection of bottles in the $200-$900 range. Most of all, you get a crowd that doesn't blink at the prices, delivering the verdict "Preston is toast" while whistling up the grand Bordeaux featured as the nightly "house red," 1995 Château Prieuré-Lichine at $12 the glass. These are folks whose conversation excludes any reference to the demise of the Crow rate, the time-honoured grain subsidy that was Ottawa's most visible support of western agriculture for decades. Their vision of rural Alberta is something that whizzes by at 140 km/h on the way to Banff or the United States. As talk turns to Day's chances, "our tax policy will get us 40 seats in Ontario for sure," there's a sense of audacity and pride in the voices.

This time, they exude the confidence that they've got it right. One more meeting to confirm Day's leadership, and the Alliance will be on its way to power. At long last, Canada will follow Calgary's lead in choosing a party that will get government out of the way as Alberta's surging economy leads Canada's remarkable run of prosperity. It's the smart, cocky, cosmopolitan face of this Alliance crowd that sets it apart from previous manifestations of Western alienation. And when you take note of the assured, edgy demeanour of people who seem to believe they are born to lead, you wonder just what it is they are alienated from.

The alchemy of the new "western alienation" is found most strongly then in Calgary. It weds the old alienation represented in resentment and long memories of repression, to the new alienation born in a sense of exceptionalism. It neatly blends two streams of resentment that are quite different, one rooted in older rural grievances of the past, the other in the impatience of a new generation that wants the political power that should go with its economic clout. It is reflected in part by the flavour of the month in western alienation in the late winter and spring of 2001, the Calgary-centric Canadian Alliance campaign to build a "firewall" to keep out external influences and protect the newfound riches. The firewall thesis was drafted by Stephen Harper, who was to succeed Day as national leader in the spring of 2002 to become the Alliance's next Great Hope. It would be wrong to evoke from the singularity of Calgary any sort of general conclusion about the disaffection of the West as a whole, or indeed about the other metropolitan centres. Yet many influential people in the four largest Western metro cities contrast their civic polity to what is perceived to be a sclerotic centre-east rooted in French-English squabbles. Stereotypes can be useful as broad descriptions, yet there are fundamental flaws in the supposition that people in the West feel the same level of anger and resentment towards the federal government. The four western provinces are in fact quite different from each other. Visionary pragmatists (no more of a contradiction than sovereignty-association) have governed Manitoba, Saskatchewan and more recently Alberta, and the NDP and Social Credit strains of prairie populism manifested themselves differently in each. British

Columbia has a tradition of "distinct society" premiers from Amor de Cosmos to W.A.C. Bennett to Dave Barrett to Glen Clark.

This political experimentation may be most visible in British Columbia, but it is organically western. The common urban western bond, so much reflected in the growing confidence of Calgary, is to embrace new solutions to traditional problems. Liberals and Conservatives are primarily parties with roots in central and eastern Canada, parties that have existed and flourished long before the West was settled. In the past century, the political history of the West has been a quixotic one, to breed parties that represented the region in a way that the Grits and Tories could not. From the Progressives to the United Farmers, the Cooperative Commonwealth Federation to Social Credit, from the Western Canada Concept to the Saskatchewan Party, the West has spawned more new political movements than any other part of the country. In order to lead within Canada, the West may have to abandon the older resentments and the culture of protest it has nurtured for decades.

Westerners need to recognise that an ever-more-prosperous and urban region cannot pretend to be a victim while its wealth and influence grow.

Much of the old alienation born from anger is a direct response to the changes wrought by technology, globalisation and indeed modernity itself. It is a reaction to the coming together of diverse peoples, shifting economies and many cultures.

Small wonder then the insecure may even turn to talk of western separation. Their unease flows from the idea that "our"' culture is under siege, that unsettling and unwanted changes can and must be turned back. Sometimes they can, but too often they can't. There is a good deal of self-deception among people who say they will keep their culture "as it always has been," inoculate their monocultural existence from infection by outside influences. This is the very heart of the atavistic western alienation that is rooted in, but not confined to, rural areas and smaller urban centres. The atavism will prove difficult to address quickly and resolutely, because mythology has its own strength and endurance.

The older face of western alienation may be a pan-Canadian phenomenon in the broader hinterland belonging to the twelve largest Canadian Census Metropolitan Areas. As most Canadians increasingly live in large urban islands dotted across an immense geography, the life of those outside the cities becomes materially and significantly different from the metropolitan one. The rural disaffected of the West may have more in common with the folks of the Annapolis Valley, the Gaspe and the Outaouais than is initially imagined.

The western provinces, with their willingness to try new approaches, recognise the new challenges of governance and step up to meet them. In a real sense, they are the vanguard of the Demotic Society. They are the place where the mingling of cultures builds the next Canada, a Canada that will indeed be a consensus of radical moderates, notwithstanding the detours through the Reform Party, the Canadian Alliance, and other futile efforts to break the tribal duality of the old partisan politics of Central Canada. The issues born in the West, the concerns raised in the West, have become part of the Demotic discourse. And as we can readily see, the very absence of the French-English debate enables us to create a vigorous Demotic dialogue.

Western provinces constitute Canada's vanguard in globalisation, and all of Canada has aspirations to be the world's vanguard nation. Our abundant resource base and our capacity to add talent and value to human resources through education, skills training and mass immigration truly enables the West to be leaders in the borderless world. We know it would be tragic to squander this potential and this opportunity for Western Canada to lead the Rest of Canada to the nation's rightful place of global leadership by combining the opportunities flowing from the highest quality of life on the planet.

It is part of the Western frustration that the Demotic search for workable pan-Canadian solutions has not permeated the national agenda to a sufficient degree.

If the ever-adaptable Demotic discourse of the West – it is always open to shaping through further debate – is adapted as a matter of national discourse, it may help us to recognise an underlying truth, one that confused talk of alienation does not address. If one steps back and looks at the last quarter century of Canadian history, one can see that there is an abiding sense of alienation in each region. The strongest sense has been surely in Quebec, which in 1995 came within a razor-thin margin of winning a mandate to negotiate a form of national sovereignty. The alienation in Quebec is political rather than economic, yet it is interesting to note that the apogee of the secessionist movement in Quebec came at a time of record federal deficits. Whether factual or not, Quebec believed it paid more in taxes to Ottawa than it received in return; by going it alone it could do rather better than run up $35 billion deficits.

In a sense, each region is alienated from the centre, and one does not have to scratch too deeply to find it. A farmer complains bitterly of subsidized foreign competitors cutting into his livelihood, and a federal government entirely insensitive to rising input costs and low agricultural prices. That complaint sounds familiar to western ears, but it came from a farmer selling vegetables in Ottawa's Byward Market.

Every region has its own sense of alienation, yet the Liberals become

Canada's government of default, just as the Progressive Conservatives become Alberta's, because they try to shape the compromise and consensus necessary to balance competing and sometimes conflicting interests in a vast country. They come closest to capturing the impulses of the Demotic Society, because they are the most open to building consensus. Nobody was necessarily delighted to return the Liberals to power a third time, nor was there any strong alternative to Premier Klein in his third victory –what other Demotic choice was there?

A small but telling illustration of how the New West is perceived speaks volumes about the character of its cities, and how the urban cities of Western Canada host the acceleration of cultural mingling, a smashing of homogeneity. The popular Japanese cookery show *Iron Chef*, a cult favourite among connoisseurs in the many countries where it is translated and aired, recently featured a first: Canadian chef Michael Noble (a Calgarian then cooking in the celebrated Diva restaurant in Vancouver), in a one-hour culinary duel with Masaharu Morimoto, judged by *Iron Chef* producers as the greatest living exponent of Japanese cuisine. The show has the chefs preparing dishes from an ingredient revealed to them just before the contest begins, and challengers hardly ever beat the "Iron Chef" in any of the styles of cuisine. Asked for his impression of Canadian cuisine, Morimoto (fittingly for the borderless world, he is head chef at Nobu, one of the most celebrated restaurants in New York City) said, "it is far more sophisticated than American cuisine" and "ranks right up there with the French." The tasting panel praised Noble's innovative mixture of Japanese and Canadian ingredients, such as wasabi radish with mascarpone cheese to flavour a smoked salmon and potato napoleon.

"This is typical of Canada, to show so much sensitivity and respect to our culture, and to make something completely new and different," said Dr. Yukio Hattori, chair of the tasting panel. Asked who would win, Noble said beforehand "we both will" because "whenever two chefs get together, they learn from one another."

This meeting of cultures is a vivid illustration of the Urban West's approach to the globalised world, and how it is received and perceived by our Asian interlocutors. Noble was invited because returning Japanese tourists raved about his cooking in Vancouver. Culinary diplomacy thus became part of the "soft power" of the world of global trade.

Our Western Canadian metro cities amount to post-modern spaces built with populations from the world over, contributing not only to a sense of "can-do" confidence, but to the very real feeling that the next Canada is being built right now in the West. This is a positive, dynamic energy that will serve the entire country well, if the older Canada reaches out to embrace the newer one. The Western cities' sense of exceptionalism is not unique. Toronto, Ottawa, Montreal are also metropolitan cities of the global economy, driven by that same feeling of being far ahead of the pack, waiting for the rest of the country to catch up. They will not necessarily submit to a political formula built on the assumption that the West is destined to lead the rest of Canada to a radiant future. Yet that too is an attitude that might change, as the older cities understand that the "founding nation" vision is more apt as an historic description, that it is one more myth to be abandoned. If the Old Canada can do so, we might even dare to add to Gilles Vigneault's evocation:

Mon pays ce n'est pas un pays c'est l'avenir
My country is not a country it's the Future.

WHY THE NEIGHBOURS
WOULD RATHER STAY HOME

IF HAPPINESS COMES TO THOSE WHO WAIT, THE "MAGIC Kingdom" at Florida's Walt Disney World certainly lives up to its billing as the "happiest place on Earth." Even in early March in 2000, in what might have been a foreshadowing of the farcical presidential election count that would unfold months later on these shores, you wait and wait and wait. Yet the never-ending line has its own attraction, allowing for the observation and reflection if not the rest a vacation is supposed to bring. It is altogether astonishing, when you think of what sheer American hucksterism and the power of the dollar has made of swamp and scrubland, of what was once a desultory place of alligators and citrus plantations, a finger of America plunging to the tropics. To turn these briny and dangerous scrublands into the most-promoted tourist attraction in the United States speaks to the heady blend of money and imagination that fuels America's successes and excesses. This was once the realm of their Catholic Majesties in Madrid, claimed and defended by the grand fleets of the Admiral of the Ocean-Sea, the first enduring economic foothold in the New World. The first landowning barons cultivated cane sugar, and these cañaveral gave their name to the cape whence rockets carried Americans to the moon.

Florida, Spanish for the flowering land, eventually fell to the Anglophone maw of the American empire. And English it remains in Disney's grand vision, especially so in the flawless English of the many Hispanics who are making Florida a beachhead in the second Spanish conquest of America. There are lakes of murky water with manicured white-sand beaches. There are lovely stretches of green, brilliant displays of flowers, an Eden of the imagination hewn from an indifferent landscape. That, and the rides – some thrilling, some tame, each with its own line up. Everywhere you turn, there is a place to eat and a place to shop, and the exit from every attraction seems to take you straight into another display of things to buy. This is the allure of the United States on the grand scale, a persuasive showcase for the combined power of money and the human imagination. The audacity of Disney is to recast the common fantasies and legends of childhood into a proprietary mould, to take ownership of what were once folk tales, and to invent a few legends of its own along the way. The Disney characters are so pervasive that you wonder how many children know A.A. Milne's original stories about Winnie-the-Pooh and Tigger, let alone Charles Perrault's magical tales of Cinderella, The Beauty and The Beast, and The Beauty Asleep in the Woods.

This myth making is very much the heart of American culture, an incessant drive to build things newer, better and bigger than anything in the Old Order. The revolutionary impulse in the American experience remains a powerful current: always moving forward, convinced that the better world remains to be built. It's a deeply ingrained impulse. Central Florida is the minimum wage capital of America; the 75,000 people who work at Disney get $5.90 an hour, or $6.25 an hour if they're experienced. So do the hundreds of thousands who work in all the tourism services spawned by the presence of Disney, Universal Studios and other theme parks. "Because I work here, I can get great discounts," says a woman, who is required to smile as she helps people get a Disney "fast pass" reservation for a ride. And yes, it's necessary to work two jobs to make ends meet, but the children are grown up, either finishing college or in a professional job. She, like several others I ask, intends to vote Republican. We are staying in what is billed as the biggest two-storey motel in the world, a functional and comfortable place in a numbing array of moderately priced inns and mass-market places to eat and shop. Driving around, you realize there is not so much a choice of places to go to, as the same choice repeated over and over: the same franchises, from Red Lobster to Wendy's, over and over again. One night, looking for Mexican food, we had to drive 25 kilometres to find a Mexican restaurant that's something other than a Taco Bell. This is American unity carried to an absurd extreme, the same suburban sprawl repeated at regular intervals. It is part of the superficial homogeneity of the United States, a deceptive sameness that covers a country as richly diverse as any immigrant-built society.

The overarching sense of a common American destiny, the loyalty to the flag and the constitutionally enshrined pursuit of happiness, nurture the notion that unity comes above all. It is a far cry from our society, in which the seams and stitches are all too visible, where the very presence of Quebec persuades us to rethink our country and challenges and prevents any enforced unity. You can see the need for the myth in a country forged by revolution. The long-ago experience of throwing off the colonial yoke is revived and nurtured by subsequent generations, instilled into newcomers as part of the essential American experience. Yet beneath the unifying myths and corporate sameness lies America's secret soul. Like ours, theirs is an immigrant country, with the infinite variety conferred by cultural mingling. For all the insistence on the primacy of English, for all the Yankee Protestant glory of the Stars and Stripes and Uncle Sam, America's secret soul sometimes speaks in all the world's tongues and follows all the world's faiths.

Most of all, it speaks in Spanish and enjoys the culture that arose from communities where Catholicism was the only faith. The prevalence of Spanish is startling, all the more so because it is a clandestine bilingualism. It is difficult to perceive, because of the diversity of the Hispanic world, in its ethnic and cultural and racial melange. En route to Ecuador in the fall of 1999 I had several hours to pass in Miami Airport, stopped by the barbershop, found several men behind the chairs. They were all white Europeans by the look of them, and spoke English with an elusive accent that definitely wasn't of the south, but could have come out of any of a half a dozen places in the US Midwest. I had arrived about the same time as another customer, who asked in Spanish how long he would have to wait. "Please," I said in my rudimentary Spanish, offering the next chair. As though a switch was thrown, the atmosphere changed at once. Everyone started speaking in Spanish, the façade of reserve melted away, and I had to apologize because my Spanish takes only a few words to turn into French. "It's nothing," said the barber cutting my hair. "We can still understand." They were Cuban, every one of them. I asked about the change in mood. "In English, you know, it's hard to be yourself, to talk normally," he explains. "North Americans, they're so busy; they're in a hurry. It's all money, money." After thirty-eighty years in the United States, he still sees himself as Hispanic in a sea of *Norteamericanos*, which seems a bit jarring in the face of the official American mythology of the melting pot. Then it turns out that in his view everyone non-Hispanic is a *Norteamericano*, including people like me, Americans of African and Asian ancestry, even people with Italian or Greek roots. I point out that there are many black people who speak Spanish. "Sure, mister. We are all Hispanic. It's the way we think, the attitude."

I see some of that attitude in a trip to New York as Canada prepares to challenge the United Nations Security Council to get beyond its veto-wielding and paralysis. Arriving tired and dehydrated from the airport just before midnight, I go into a fast-food place for iced tea. The people behind the counter are white and black, but they're speaking Spanish with one another. I ask for a receipt in Spanish, eyes light up, and my money is waved away: "Next time." At Zarelas, a crowded and extremely trendy Mexican restaurant in midtown Manhattan – a sauce made with mashed pumpkin seeds and roasted avocado leaves is a revelation – a few words in Spanish produce a table where there seemed to be none. You come to realize that there's more to this than linguistic solidarity; it's a celebration of the bilingualism and multiculturalism that Official America denies, with its blinding mythology and its English-only language policies. In our motel just outside the sprawling Disney property, I've been speaking English at breakfast all week. I decide to express my thanks in Spanish to a particularly solicitous waiter. The "have a good day sir" of English becomes the Spanish: "Do you need more juice cups for the girls? No? Enjoy yourselves, my brother."

"Canada and the United States are very different countries," says my friend Paul, who worked as a Canadian diplomat in Washington for five years and is married to an American doctor. "Because we share a language with them, so many Canadians think they know the

States. But it's a huge country, a diverse country, different from us in so many ways that only become clear when you live here.

"There are things to admire, things to deplore, but we're not the same."

The vibrant cultural diversity of America is reflected in its local politics, but seldom at the highest national levels. On Super Tuesday, a sporting nickname Americans apply to a cluster of primary elections in their hideously extended presidential election campaign, a new mythology is being crafted. This is the image of likely Republican nominee George W. Bush as the outsider, the underdog, and the champion who overcame strong odds to emerge triumphant. This image, so central to revolution, sits uncomfortably on the bland and vague Bush. On this night, he has comprehensively defeated his more lively rival, the former prisoner of war John McCain. In the Republican field, McCain seemed the more likely source of myth – quite apart from the image of the warrior triumphant, Caesar returned to Rome from a harsh battle, he had much more life and juice than Bush. McCain revels in a life full of its share of hootin' and hollerin' while his pinched-faced conqueror busily tries to paper over a past when he drank and shouted and maybe, just maybe, tasted coca that didn't come in a bottle.

Of the Bush boys, the sons of the former president who have made it big in politics, the Boy Jeb comes across rather better than his older brother. Jeb is the governor of Florida, and he seems to have an instinctive understanding of the potential power of Hispanic America, soon to become the largest minority in the United States. Both the Bush boys speak Spanish. Yet it's Jeb who's building a career with the backing of Florida's large Hispanic population. He's championing a favourite right-wing agenda, the end of affirmative action programs that level the playing field for blacks and other minorities. He calls his campaign One Florida, and he has strong support from the Hispanic community, which has by and large flourished. The largest civil rights march in Florida's history converges on the state capital Tallahassee, but the Boy Jeb is unmoved. The crowd of marchers is largely black with a significant white presence, but there are hardly any Hispanics at all. Jeb knows better than his brother that in the long run, keeping the loyalty of a growing Hispanic power base makes more sense than catering to a narrower and older right-wing of so-called conservative Christians.

Yet the evidence of one's eyes shows that affirmative action has worked. In New York as in Florida one sees a significant population of middle-class blacks. Far from the media perception of blacks as either millionaire entertainers/athletes or perpetrator/victims of crime, the emergence of what is today called an African-American (Martin Luther King Jr. hated the phrase, by the way, ringingly declaring that no one was going to question his Americanism by adding the word African) middle class is impressive proof that there are dividends to be found in levelling the playing field.

As Bill Clinton points out, though, the liberating policies of civil rights and affirmative action weren't only concerned with emancipating black Americans. For the first time in his presidency, the man labelled by the poet Maya Angelou as "America's first black president" took part this month in the annual commemoration of a seminal civil rights march in Selma, Alabama. For a rare moment, he transcended politics as he said he too was kept prisoner by America's own version of apartheid. "You set me free."

Clinton spoke not so much of the position of privilege he enjoys today, but of the poverty-ridden, dysfunctional home in which he was raised. To be poor and white in the South, where the reigning mythology held that whites were inherently superior to blacks was to be an outcast – almost as though you had let down your race by daring to be in the same poverty to which nearly all blacks were consigned. A moment like that, even seen on television from a Florida motel room brings a flash of insight. It explains the connection between Clinton and all those folks working for $5.90 an hour, eating fast-food and southern barbecue, living in apartments or modest homes well away from wealth. In spirit – if not in material circumstance – he is still one of them. This is really where he came from, from a life of poverty where hope was the only free commodity. The difference between then and now is the construction of a robust American economy wherein people are able to hold more than one minimum-wage job, and the ready availability of mass consumer goods which enable even the working poor to have many of the material trappings their wealthier counterparts enjoy. Even those minimum-wage workers who told me they'll vote Republican cannot share the Boy George's moral outrage about Clinton. They understand the idea of taking what they can get. Unlike the establishment – outraged that someone from the working classes actually rose up to become president – they know that one of their own made good. Clinton, for all the sleaze and scandal of his personal behaviour, embodies more clearly than any politician of his generation that America is indeed a place where ordinary citizens can fulfil all of their dreams. And after a golden sunset over a landscape of dreams, watching a majestic display of fireworks burst above "Cinderella's Castle," you can almost believe that it's true.

In a fundamental sense, that is the limit of American ambition. Their global leadership flows from a sense of exporting consumerism, the pursuit of material gain, and the chase after wealth as a means to happiness. That's why the neighbours are going to stay home, as Canada and others try to create a global culture of peace. The American view of the world is not so much as a realm of possibilities beyond mere economic gain, but as a place full of threats and fury, out to "get" America if it's not vigilant. Ironically, the vigilance fails closest to home – while the giddy crowds swirled at Disney World, a determined group of Saudis took the flying lessons that anyone could buy in Florida, all the better to manoeuvre commercial jets into public buildings. The search for an external threat is part of the thinking behind the missile defence shield first proposed by Ronald Reagan and now revived by the Boy George in the first hours of his tainted accession to the US presidency. At stake is not so much the viability of the missile defence system as the $90 billion the US has already pumped in to the research and development for the so-called shield. Until the terrorist attacks on the World Trade Center and the Pentagon, this insular dream remained intact. Yet the shattering of that domestic confidence resulted in what was essentially a police action against the Taliban regime of Afghanistan, with the support of the United Nations. Had it not been for the strike at the very heart of US power, the US may not have played any role in an international campaign against a pariah regime in Afghanistan. Had the terror attack targeted another country, perhaps a NATO ally like Britain or Germany, the US might at most have played the more limited role it favoured in the Clinton years – launching bombs and cruise missiles from afar, rather than actually putting troops at risk on the ground.

Indeed, the exposed vulnerability of the US to determined terrorists gave a prescience to Axworthy's blunt and incisive critique of the United States' plan to build the costly and unproven defence project, when he appeared at the UN Security Council during Canada's 1999-2001 tenure. It doesn't stop cruise missiles. It doesn't stop drones. It can't detect missiles launched at sea. Most of all, it doesn't stop the determined terrorist with a suitcase-sized nuclear warhead – the kind you can fly in as hand luggage in a business-class seat, let alone the one who flies an aircraft into a public building.

The Clinton presidency tried to put the missile defence aside, and to enter into some limited engagements with the world that went beyond militarism and commerce. With the second Bush presidency, there was every indication before 11 September 2001 that the US was going to stay home, protect what it has, and only engage with the world if there is a clear advantage to the US in doing so. This notion of engagement was a throwback to the days when the threat of nuclear war came in a mutually annihilating exchange of intercontinental ballistic missiles. That fantasy ended quickly. Even though there are plans for a missile defence still, the US leadership is more ready to acknowledge that a fuller and more comprehensive engagement is essential. The events in Afghanistan, the combination of chasing down terrorists while creating coalitions to rebuild civil society, marks a new endeavour for the US. This, in turn, gives Canada an opening, as we shall see in the concluding chapter, to influence the US to make a more positive contribution to the world.

The pre-Afghanistan attitude of the US etched a vivid contrast between two competing versions of how the world ought to evolve. In our approach, Canada works in partnership with the United Nations, NATO and like-minded countries to promote human rights, social development and a farewell to arms. The early months of the Bush presidency adhered to an older view of security – one built on loyalty to the defence agenda of the United States military and the industrial complex that benefits from it, and belief in the necessity of keeping a strong nuclear deterrent. Indeed, that combined sense of isolationism and exceptionalism led Bush's administration to withdraw from five major international treaties in the first months of his presidency. It was a robust demonstration that the United States could set itself apart, chart its own vision of how history ought to unfold, withdraw from a broader engagement with the world. The difficulty is that far too often, the US engagement in the world has been limited to economics alone. Given a choice, the neighbours would rather stay home, in the Magic Kingdom of their creation, seeing the world as a place separate and apart from them.

All of that changed on 11 September 2001. When the terrorists flew commercial airlines into the World Trade Center and the Pentagon, it was in a very real sense the end of the Magic Kingdom. Not only did an age of innocence vanish, so did the sense that America can afford to stand apart from the world. Much good was achieved in the times when the United States took seriously its responsibility to make a positive contribution to the world. The Peace Corps of the 1960s, the Marshall Plan after the Second World War, stand out as instances of the positive effects of a committed US involvement in building civil society. If the US comes to see that mere economic globalisation is not enough, it will acknowledge there is a role and indeed a demand for a broader and more positive American influence in shaping a better world. The US may come to accept that if we are to collectively succeed in addressing the scourge of terrorism, we need a clear understanding of what it will take to build human security, and how that must be grounded in a culture of peace.

The New Frontiers
of Peace

There is a momentous opening now for Canada to lead the future by shaping the new frontiers of peace, because this is a time when the United Nations itself is looking for answers. Kofi Annan's tenure as secretary general evokes values that echo Canada's own sense of self. It was clearly set out in an April 1988 speech by Annan in Berkeley.

> The evolution of United Nations peacekeeping from the traditional kind of patrolling buffer zones and cease-fire lines to the modern, more complex manifestations in the former Yugoslavia has been neither smooth nor natural. It has created conceptual confusions and inflated expectations, betrayed hopes and blemished reputations. It has made us review our responsibilities and question our most basic assumptions about the very nature of war and the very high price of peace in the post-cold war era," Annan said in what is now recognised as a pioneering assessment of the new frontiers of peace.

Peacekeepers were asked the impossible, and sometimes, therefore, even failed to achieve the possible. Should we, in Rwanda, have done more to prevent the catastrophe? Should we have been able to seize the arms caches and eliminate the threat to the Tutsi population from the Hutu extremists when they began their campaign of genocide? With hindsight, yes. Should we, in Bosnia, have been able to prevent the safe areas from falling and protected the population of Srebrenica from terror and death at the hands of their enemies? Of course. But could we, in either of these cases, have done so, with the means and mandate at hand? Absolutely not. Any assessment of United Nations peacekeeping must begin with this recognition, if its credibility and legitimacy is to be restored. No one laments the tragic incidents of Bosnia and Rwanda more than we at the United Nations do. We were asked to step in when all others had failed, and when no power or alliance equipped to act on behalf of the world had the political will to do so. When global opinion calls for the world to 'do something' about a crisis, we become the 'doers', whether we have been given the tools or not."

Two years and a fortnight after Annan's landmark speech at Berkeley, a smaller-than-planned deployment of United Nations peacekeepers-cum-peacemakers, lacking the tools they had been promised, found themselves face to face with a potential catastrophe. Indian General

Vijay Jetley commanded a largely pan-African UN force that was preparing the ground for what was planned to become the largest ever deployment in UN history. In Sierra Leone, armed with a standard cease-fire mandate offered by the Security Council on 22 October 1999, Jetley enjoyed a more robust mandate sanctioned on 7 February 2000, enabling the soldiers under his command to actually begin building a peace rather than merely monitoring a cease-fire. They were in the front lines of a conflict within a nation, the model of warfare that has become more common than the conflict between nations that marked the first UN peacekeeping mandates.

Until the first days of May, it appeared that success was in sight. Yet the peace was nearly undone by the madness of Foday Sankoh, leader of the Revolutionary United Front, whose army of child soldiers had been singularly successful in spreading terror and chaos. Sent to guarantee a peace in the aftermath of Sierra Leone's civil war, charged with creating a climate wherein civil society and civil institutions could be rebuilt, Gen. Jetley's peacekeepers faced a virulent recurrence of the conflict that had ruined a potentially prosperous country in Anglophone West Africa.

There was no logical reason why this should be so – Sankoh had not given up control of the illicit diamond trade that fuelled his rebellion, and he had a role in government. The hard-won peace covered by the UN mandate seemed as durable as any in the immediate aftermath of a conflict. Civil wars are inherently illogical, yet when they end with a peace accord that shares power and gives each party some of the responsibility for governance, one might believe that there is some basis for building a peace. This had certainly been the thinking amongst the members of the United Nations and the Security Council, which had authorised a sufficiently large force – in excess of

11,000 soldiers, and many civilians and volunteers – to establish peace in Sierra Leone.

Stung by the lessons of Rwanda exactly six years earlier, haunted by the madness of the carnage in the civil war in Sierra Leone's neighbour Liberia in the latter half of the 1990s, the UN determined that it could not afford to stand by yet again in an African conflict. In the internal politics of the United Nations, there was a stark contrast drawn between the resources diverted to address the European conflict in the Balkans in the 1990s, and the lack of both political will and resources in quelling African conflicts. Indeed, in the aftermath of the Central African debacle in April 1994, there was clear evidence that the United Nations had repeatedly ignored the warnings of Canadian General Romeo Dallaire that a slaughter was imminent in Rwanda. Faced with genocide, taking the bodies of dead peacekeepers with them, the small UN contingent fled Rwanda. The burden of failure, the inability to stop the genocide of half a million people, was too much for Dallaire to bear.

The United Nations Under-secretary General who gave insufficient weight to Dallaire's warnings also took the lesson to heart – Kofi Annan would not make the same mistake again. This time, peace would not only be kept, but also nourished and allowed to grow. Sierra Leone, then, was to be the fruit of Lessons Learned – the UN would provide proper resources, and a large enough force, and lay the post-war foundations to rebuild a country that ranked dead last on the United Nations Development Programme's Human Development Index.

The UN thought it had time – although most of the peacekeepers on the ground in May 2000 were mainly Nigerian and Kenyan and Zambian, a larger international contingent was on the way. The inclusion of both parties to the civil war in government – including the rebel leader Foday Sankoh, released from a death sentence under his onetime

Nigerian captors – brought the hope that armed forces might be disarmed and displaced populations returned to their homes.

Despite all the preparation and all the hopes, 500 UN peacekeepers hampered by a mandate to return fire only in self-defence found themselves the captives of drug-fed boys and teenagers in early May. Of the many eventualities the UN had anticipated, it had perhaps taken too lightly the probability that Foday Sankoh suffered from a serious mental illness. He heard voices. These voices told him to resume the war. And the children and teens he led looked to him as a messianic force.

And so it was that an armed force animated by a leader who hears voices threatened to unravel the entire UN mission in Sierra Leone, to send it packing just as Dallaire's woefully small force had been forced to flee Rwanda – despite Annan's assurances that lessons had indeed been learned.

Yet the mission did not collapse, thanks to sheer luck. Rather than fleeing after the mass abduction of 500 of its members, the UN forces regrouped around the capital Freetown. They were aided by troops who were in no way part of the Security Council mandate – a contingent of British paratroops originally brought in to evacuate British nationals and foreigners from its former colony.

Foday Sankoh's rebels ignored the peace accord their leader had signed and resumed the battle. Caught well short of the full deployment of international troops authorised by the Security Council, the UN mission was bolstered by the presence of the paratroops, an unexpected bonus.

Sankoh's murderous brigade of child and teen-aged soldiers, in scenes reminiscent of the Children's Crusade that began the last millennium, had spent several years rampaging through the countryside, hacking off limbs, shooting whom they wished. Even though they were repelled from the capital, victory for the government was by no means assured, until the second stroke of luck. On 17 May 2000 government forces captured Sankoh. More of the UN hostages were released. More international troops began to arrive; the contingent was to be 17,000 – the largest international peace force ever assembled. By half-measures, in response to imminent disaster, the UN was able to assemble the numbers one needs to sustain a credible military presence.

Yet the Sierra Leone crisis is not necessarily a story with a happy outcome. The UN was fortunate, but it should not have been in a position to depend on luck and happenstance to assure the success of its missions. It pointed out the crying need for the UN standing army sought by Annan's predecessor Boutros Boutros-Ghali. The Boutros-Ghali call for a UN military presence, perhaps a rapid deployment force, wasn't only about numbers. An effective military intervention, particularly in the cause of restoring order and laying the foundations for peace building, needs a sense of purpose and cohesion. That most frequently comes from training together, living together, building the fraternal bonds between individual soldiers that enable mutual trust under fire. Moreover, it enables a common standard of training for UN peacekeepers, and allows for the integration of command structures. A war zone is not the ideal place to mesh different commands, to forge unity amongst soldiers from different countries and cultures. This is better done away from the theatres of conflict. Peacekeepers and peacebuilders need to train together and work together before they are sent to contain a crisis. Sierra Leone, like Somalia before it, demonstrates the dangers and the futility of trying to cobble together a cohesive presence on the fly.

The theme Annan so vigorously raised in his Berkeley speech and indeed in at least a dozen major addresses of his secretary-generalship rang truer than ever – the UN needs the proper resources and the proper mandate to keep and build peace. The theme is repeated in the August 2000 peace-keeping review from a UN select committee: a stable and predictable roster of troops available for deployment, and the necessary funding to elevate UN intervention from rhetorical ideal to a workable reality.

In a world accustomed to war, the imperatives of peace building represent new ground, with a paucity of resources and an absence of clear direction. Building and sustaining a peace takes the international community into new areas: into violating the sovereignty of other nations, of ignoring territorial integrity, demanding the right to act aggressively against governments that violate the Universal Declaration of Human Rights. It is a remaking of the world order made possible by the end of the Cold War between the western alliance and the former Soviet Empire. In theory at least it promises a future wherein human rights are paramount. It flows from an evolving idea of human security – the notion that human rights transcend political boundaries. With more and more conflicts within nations rather than between nations – civil war rather than wars between countries – protecting civilians in armed conflict becomes the priority. That was the overriding mandate in Sierra Leone when the peacekeepers went in, and the necessity of building a peace is greatly abetted by Sankoh's capture. Yet in the days of the Cold War, it would have been unthinkable for the UN or indeed any collection of democracies to embark on a robust intervention for the stated purpose of upholding human rights. NATO's bombing of the former Yugoslavia as it intervened in the civil war in the rebellious Serbian province of Kosovo was a turning point. It marked the first large-scale decision by western democracies to violate a country's borders and its national sovereignty in the name of rescuing people from the persecution directed against them by their own government. This illegal and unilateral measure – the bombing was conducted without the authorisation of the Security Council – did not sit well with many countries, because one of the founding tenets of the United Nations is that national borders are inviolate.

Had Sierra Leone indeed ended in catastrophe, the isolationists in the United States surely would have seen this as yet another sign of UN failure. It would have bolstered them in their fundamental thinking that the UN was not to be trusted, that America's sense of exceptionalism should lead it to act alone. Wealth and technology created a new hubris in the US in particular and the North Atlantic Treaty Organisation alliance in general. It was the belief that policing the world ought to be achieved with no loss of life on the part of US and Western forces. The NATO bombing of former Yugoslavia in its Balkan intervention, the use of long-range cruise missiles in the Gulf War, the unleashing of the latest technologies of warfare, fuelled the thought that peacekeeping ought to come without risk. That all changed with the Afghanistan campaign. Until US troops pursued Osama bin Laden's followers on the ground, US foreign policy was to avoid messy situations that actually put troops at risk – the Republicans in the US Congress seriously intended to cut off funding for UN peacekeepers in Kosovo in the summer of 2000.

This attitude deeply influenced the US conduct of its membership in the Security Council. And in turn it contributed to the general impasse amongst the five veto-bearing permanent members of the Security Council – the US, Russia, China, France and Britain. The serious answer to Annan's recurring analysis – the provision of adequate funding, troops and indeed a proper mandate – was nowhere to be seen. The UN crisis in Sierra Leone in May 2000 shows that the western democracies and other nations that are much more adept at fighting wars have yet to learn the imperatives of building a peace. Moreover, Sankoh's readiness to ignore treaties he himself had signed offers a classic illustration of the difficulty of peace building, of trying to establish order and civil society in the chaotic aftermath of civil war. The central dilemma – in a world where $1.5 trillion flows annually into "defence" spending, preparations for war fighting and the legal portion of the global arms trade – is determining who pays for peace. The United Nations is chronically hampered by a lack of funds. The annual budget for all UN operations, all agencies and programmes, is about that of a medium-sized Canadian province – smaller than the annual budget of the Province of Alberta. Indeed, the chronic shortage of funding for a basket of grand demands and aspirations led Annan to propose a "Global Compact," wherein business and enterprises would be sub-contracted to provide and perhaps pay for services the United Nations would normally offer.

The question of who pays sits front and centre: not just in properly funding the campaign in Sierra Leone, but in the two theatres where the UN has two of the broadest mandates in history.

The United Nations was in 2000 *de iure* and *de facto* the government of two territories emerging from conflict, Kosovo and East Timor, although its hold on Kosovo is more tenuous than it ought to be. In each case, lack of money eroded the lofty goal of establishing a lasting peace, rooted in a civil society. As former Czech foreign minister Jiri Dienstbier famously put it after a visit to the Serbian province of Kosovo in the former Yugoslavia in the fall of 1999, the spring ethnic cleansing of Albanians has been replaced by the fall ethnic cleansing of Serbs. As with the near-debacle in Sierra Leone, the UN's difficulties in restoring civil society in Kosovo aptly illustrate the challenges of peacebuilding, the next step after traditional peacekeeping establishes a cease-fire.

Sustainable peace is new and unknown territory for the UN and the international community. It was one of the first items on Annan's plate when he assumed the UN's highest office, and he took a much more expansive view of peace than its minimalist definition as the absence of war. "Lasting peace requires more than intervention of the Blue Helmets on the ground," Annan told the World Economic Forum in February 1997. "Effective peacekeeping demands a broader notion of human security. We cannot be secure amidst starvation, we cannot build peace without alleviating poverty, and we cannot build freedom on foundations of injustice."

Yet that broad vision can only flow from a narrower mission: the requirement to end a conflict so that the foundations of justice can be established. Both tasks are necessary, Annan has consistently stressed that the UN can't do it alone. It should not be expected to "do something" in every outbreak, nor should its inability to act be condemned and dismissed as an ineffectual stance. The world body cannot impose a miraculous settlement, nor can it reasonably expected to build a peace if there is no organic desire to end a conflict. "Political motivation and political persuasion are critical elements in a peace process," Annan told a peacekeeping seminar in November 1997. "When the parties are genuinely interested in a settlement, mountains can be moved in the interest of peace. However, in chaotic conditions in which power has devolved to splinter factions, which have no real interest in peace, there are palpable limits to what the international community can accomplish. A sense of community – the will to reconcile – cannot be imposed."

Those words certainly ring true in Kosovo. The UN felt compelled to try, because it was given the task of protecting civilians in the territory after NATO's bombs stopped the rampage of Slobodan Milosevic against his rebellious province. Milosevic's subsequent ouster in October 2000 – and the establishment of a government headed by Vojislav Kostunica – may have been a direct result of the NATO intervention. Milosevic's subsequent arrest by the Kostunica government, and his delivery for trial on war crimes charges under a UN-sanctioned process, does bode well for the rule of law, but it does not necessarily enhance the prospect of a reasonable outcome in Kosovo. Even so, the very fact that elections were held in Kosovo towards the end of 2001 is a promising sign, one that could not have been anticipated just a scant few months before. Given the lack of resources available to the UN, it is a miraculous outcome, and it could easily have gone terribly wrong. Indeed, as winter yielded to the spring of 2000 in Kosovo, the United Nations continued to struggle with too little money and too few resources to stop a tide of chaos. As divided communities and divided cities flourished, the UN remained in danger of losing the war against ethnic hatred. Even as municipal elections brought a measured attempt at formalising the construction of civil society in Kosovo in the fall of 2000, the fundamental menace of ethnic vengeance had yet to abate. The UN had to plead with the now dominant Albanians to respect the civil rights of the minority Serbs. Indeed, this development gave rise to Slobodan Milosevic's extraordinary defence when he was at last brought to face an international tribunal for crimes against humanity. Milosevic said he had been fighting the very Muslim terror that targeted the US on 11 September 2001. This response to a catalogue of appalling accusations revealed quite clearly the depth of the bitterness that tumbled the Balkans into civil wars, and perhaps showed the futility of well-intentioned attempts by honest brokers to craft a peace when the belligerents had no interest or willingness in finding an accommodation.

The principal question of Milosevic and Kosovo, and indeed of every jurisdiction trying to rebuild after civil war, remains: Can peace be built without a real willingness by the combatants to work together? That's the hard reality the UN faced in Kosovo. While the UN mission is meeting limited success, is it really in a position to build a viable society? The head of the chronically impoverished Kosovo mission, Bernard Kouchner, appeared regularly in 1999 and 2000 before donor nations and the UN to ask for more money. In the absence of stable funding, Kouchner faced a daunting challenge in trying to establish a stable government – creating a civilian police, a civilian justice system, paying for teachers and engineers and medical staff to allow for parallel government structures, mostly from the officially disbanded but still functioning Kosovo Liberation Army, to take root and flourish. If the Kosovo mission were properly funded, those seeds of future conflict would not so readily germinate. Without the resources for a long-term presence, the UN can't work effectively at rebuilding lives. Where will those resources come from? Already, the world's wealthy countries are asking questions about the reconstruction of East Timor. "In the Security Council, they're asking if it's really worth spending $3 billion or $4 billion to build a civil society for only 850,000 people," Robert Fowler, who until the fall of 2000 was Canada's Permanent Representative to the United Nations, remarked in a conversation with the author in November 1999. The irony is that the world spends that $4 billion CDN daily on weapons and defence. In that context, peace building in Timor is surely a low cost.

By contrast, the costs of failing to build peace are enormous. This is why the Canadian agenda of building and exporting our model of civil society, taking a culture of peace to the world, is a necessity rather than a Utopian dream. The UN has kept combatants apart in Cyprus for decades. It appears as though the island will be divided between Greeks and Turks in perpetuity. How long does the UN have to keep peace there? At what cost? How much better off might Cyprus be if peacebuilding had ended the divisions? Despite the apparent success of elections, the future of Kosovo is in a holding pattern until there's a permanent political settlement. Yet the UN's peacebuilding presence, under-funded and inadequate though it may be, is better than no intervention at all. It at least permitted a return to local governance and elected representatives, even though the lingering bitterness between communities once at war does not readily abate. In East Timor, there was a genuine opportunity to "buy" a lasting peace. Even though resources for the UN operation were slow in coming, it is a true peacebuilding effort, because the Indonesian forces that occupied East Timor for twenty-five years are gone. The former Portuguese colony gained true independence on 20 May 2002 thanks to a beneficial UN presence. The UN administrator, Brazilian diplomat Sergio Vieira de Mello, was essentially empowered to make other such fundamental decisions until a properly constituted civilian government is in place. At the very least, the UN presence brought an organised response to the catastrophic spring 2000 flooding that threatened to destroy the island's $50 million coffee crop. That first act of economic assistance created an atmosphere of trust that led to the elections in the spring of 2002 to elect the first independent government of East Timor. The stability conferred by the UN presence – and the end of militarism in Indonesia's own transition to democracy – enabled East Timor to achieve a level of peace that few could have foreseen even in the mid-1990s. Indeed, the fall of the Suharto regime in Indonesia may have done more for East Timor's prospects than the UN mandate. It led in May 2002 to what would once have been unthinkable – the President of the Republic of Indonesia, Megawati Sukarnoputri, honouring with her presence the inauguration of the once-jailed rebel Xanana Gusmao as the first elected leader of the new country of East Timor.

If Kosovo represents the obstacles to peacebuilding, then East Timor represents the potential and the promise – as long as the world comes up with the money to make it work. The fact that both Kosovo and East Timor had bursts of luck and relatively happy outcomes is an admixture of good fortune, and the resolve of UN officials and indigenous administrators alike to make the best of what little they were given. Yet the UN's work in both places shows that peace building can't work unless leaders of the democratic world agree to provide the requisite money, resources and commitment. Annan's broader agenda of human security is also a cornerstone of Canadian foreign policy. It comes from a recognition that it isn't enough just to establish a truce – building a lasting peace is the only way a truce can really work. In that context, the funding for East Timor is seen as the essential investment needed to put the 850,000 Timorese on a foundation of civil society, so that they can enjoy equality of opportunity after winning their independence from Portugal and Indonesia.

When a lack of resources causes the theory of peace building to fall apart – as in Kosovo, where the drug traffickers of the officially defunct Kosovo Liberation Army were back in business in the autumn of 1999 – the limits of the UN's ability to build peace are clearly demonstrated. As vengeful attacks by Albanians against Serbs continued, the UN found it difficult to establish the credibility and trust necessary to create a society in which all the ethnic groups can co-exist. Kouchner continued to be desperately short of the cash needed to run a civilian government in the winter of 1999-2000. The situation improved a bit by mid-2000, with pledges from European governments for reconstruction loans and money to pay for the UN operations. Yet it is difficult to escape the conclusion that the lack of money comes from not a paucity of funding, but from an absence of determination. That determination may be revived as the US takes a leading role in the global fight against terrorism – defined here as acts of violence launched against civilian populations in order to destroy the intercourse of everyday life. Even so, there are clear indications that the US is not the nation that can lead the search for enduring peace. What was effectively a police action in Afghanistan against the al Qaeda movement and its Taliban allies, sanctioned by the UN, would have been nothing more than an unilateral act of revenge had the world not sided with the US. Although the American penchant for unilateralism appeared somewhat tempered in the first months of the Afghan campaign, it reasserted itself in Bush's State of the Union address in 2002. He referred to an "axis of evil" comprising states that posed more an irritation than a threat to US interests: North Korea, Iran and Iraq. As though trying to play out the unfinished fights of his father's presidency, Bush *fils* tried to expand the mandate of the international alliance fighting to support the new interim government in Afghanistan. Canada's resistance to a US-proposed war against Iraq was a quite proper response to recklessness. Saddest of all, the younger Bush seemed to lack a fundamental grasp of just how delicate a balance his diplomats had crafted in building an international coalition against al Qaeda, its leader Osama bin Laden, and the Taliban regime. While Bush's Secretary of State Colin Powell tried to keep the alliance intact, Canada and America's European allies resisted Bush's unilateral threats against Iran and Iraq. Had they not, the entire foundation of the Afghan intervention might have been swept away. Bush's actions in the first months of 2002 pointed at best to an ambiguity in America's attitudes – while it saw the necessity of building coalitions to fight fire with fire, it had no particular interest in a broader multilateral agenda, trying to build a broad coalition that would not only bring peace but build peace and sustain peace.

Indeed, Bush's enthusiastic support for the Ariel Sharon government in Israel offered another indication that the US is more comfortable with the idea of using violence to fight violence, than with the more complex and infinitely more challenging task of crafting and nourishing peace. While every country has an inalienable right to defend itself against terrorism that seeks to disrupt its very existence, there is a certain point in which the cycle of attack and retribution seems utterly pointless. That was surely the lesson offered in the spiralling bloodshed that consumed Israelis and Palestinians in the first months of the new millennium. At some point, the fighting stops out of sheer exhaustion, out of utter dismay at the human price, if not from an international intervention. Who will pick up the pieces? What happens once the big guns are silenced, and only the skirmishes remain? We asked that question throughout the 20th century, and found some promising answers. Peacekeeping, diplomacy, negotiation, the transfer of resources to abet reconstruction (as was done with post-war Germany and Japan) were 20th century solutions after the fighting stopped. In the 21st century, we shall face the task of building a peace and making it last. The art of sustaining peace may be the paramount challenge of the coming decades. And as we shall explore in the next chapter, it is here that Canada's experience, example and leadership may be most fruitfully displayed.

WHAT SECURITY
REALLY MEANS

LLOYD AXWORTHY ENDED A DISTINGUISHED CAREER AS foreign minister at the turn of the century – a career of great achievement and controversy, marked by the courage and capacity to project the ideals of Canada on to the global stage. Axworthy is the third in the great triumvirate of foreign ministers who charted Canada's place in the world in the latter half of the 20th century, and in so doing defined new possibilities for their country. It is their example, and their legacy, that enables Canada to define and evoke a culture of peace as a remedy to the conflicts of the world. And it is in the new frontiers of peace where Canada and the ideals of Canadianism will be most effective, as our country leads the future.

Lester Pearson, the creator of United Nations peacekeeping, represented the first evolution of the modern Canada – defying the great powers to chart an independent Canadian course, showing overt sympathy and identification with the newer and smaller nations of the world. Joe Clark's tenure as foreign minister was the most pivotal. He was part of the government that moved with confidence into a free-trading relationship with the United States, and carried that sense of confidence abroad as a champion of human rights, nuclear disarmament and a more peaceable world. Clark and former prime minister Brian Mulroney's singular leadership in the international campaign against apartheid was vital in hastening South Africa's transition to democracy. Axworthy built on the work of his estimable predecessors – indeed, his time as foreign minister was a natural continuum from Clark, picking up the threads dropped by less distinguished ministers in between.

All three of them redefined the meaning of the word security as it applies to nations and governments. The traditional view, based on military might and the ability to project that power swiftly and rapidly to protect national interests, has been at the heart of American definitions of security since the Second World War. This militaristic view is based on a notion of strong national defence, including threats that might be remote or unlikely: hence the idea of a space-based missile-defence system against nuclear attack. That notion of security gained even greater force in the United States in the wake of the 11 September 2001 terror attacks. Once invincibility was shattered, once vulnerability was exposed, America set out to build even stronger defences, warning a decades-long "war on terrorism" might be necessary to abolish any possibility of another such attack on US soil. In the first months after the attacks, the US government regularly issued cryptic warnings that a terror attack is imminent, and warned people to be vigilant. In the budget that followed, billions of dollars were spent on homeland defence, and no one questioned whether the US military budget should be subject to any limits on its growth. Yet as the terrorist attacks demonstrated, no amount of money or vigilance can buy absolute security. Canada's trio of eminent foreign ministers advocated a more complex sense of global security, based on mutual succour and interdependence. By the mid-

1990s, this evolved into what came to be known as human security, a notion of international peace and security based on protecting the rights of the individual. In the foreign policy that has evolved over the past two decades, Canada brings to the table a new definition of what security means – one based on the primacy of human rights, and individual well being. This means saving people caught in war, rescuing people from terror, fighting poverty, empowering people and nations, being partners in development, giving people tools to build lives of meaning and purpose. All of this should be done by transcending traditional notions of national boundaries, because individuals come first.

Axworthy's signal contribution was to revive the sense of Canadian internationalism that has always been the core of our immigrant nation, to foster the sense that we are part of a global community. He found an equal share of allies and detractors, yet there is no doubt that under his direction, Canada once again aspired to the heady reaches of global leadership. Axworthy represented one of the two seemingly contradictory faces of Prime Minister Jean Chrétien's government. One belonged to the continental free traders seeking ever-closer harmony and integration within the North American economy, accepting perforce US dominance and leadership in matters economic, content to be a satellite to the mighty planet of the US. The other, the one Axworthy best represented, appealed to a Canadian sense of internationalism. It took the view that Canada's foreign policy interests were best served by seeking alliances and coalitions with many nations. It explicitly rejected the view that US leadership and supremacy in world affairs was a good or desirable development. There is no real contradiction here. It is a recognition that economic interests are one thing, and the world beyond mere economics is quite another. When the two views came into serious conflict – as in Axworthy's support for nuclear disarmament – Chrétien sided with the US. By and large, these two dimensions of Canadianism sometimes created the perception that Canada was doing too much to annoy the US. Yet the greatest annoyance came as a result of Canadian success, not failure. The Ottawa protocol banning anti-personnel mines seemed like a Utopian dream. Yet under Axworthy's leadership, it became an international treaty. So did the statute that created the International Criminal Court, an intrusion into national sovereignty that infuriated the US. Had Axworthy failed in either of these vital initiatives, he would have been ignored as another dreamy idealist, or he would have faced derision as someone who doesn't know the difference between ideals and illusions. By turning idealism into concrete action (even with the limited resources granted him by the government he served), he invited the consternation of his critics. There is a strong resistance to any suggestion that our country could be the best at anything; that we might be better suited to chart new courses than to follow old ones; that we can indeed chart our own course in the world, without seeking the approval or the leadership of our infinitely more powerful neighbour. As I have argued throughout this book, the "best country in the world" status conferred on Canada by the United Nations Human Development Index brings with it the obligation of leadership, not a military leadership, nor a preachy or moral one. It is the quiet leadership of setting an example, of achieving something to which other nations might aspire. The obligation is to project to the world the values and visions that wrought modern Canada. And it is this projection of Canadianism – best reflected in such concepts as "soft power" and "human security" that made Axworthy especially controversial for some Canadians.

The domestic resistance to any global leadership role may arise from what is typically called a Canadian sense of modesty. Yet it may also reflect a feeling of insecurity and inadequacy – a feeling that we're not up to the demands of global leadership, a role better left to mightier countries. This attitude informed much of the discomfort with Axworthy's attempts to make Canada a leader in crafting a new notion of civil society, based on concepts like soft power and human security. The very phrases attracted much derision, especially from those who understood only the concept favoured by our southern neighbour – the "hard power" that flows from the planet's most dominant military forces. The US use of military muscle is part of its ambivalent relationship with the United Nations. In the last five decades of the 20th century, the US used the UN when their agendas coincide, and chose to go it alone when agendas advanced at the UN cam into conflict with American priorities. The former Reform Party foreign affairs critic Bob Mills led the criticism against soft power – yet even the critics mellowed. When Keith Martin succeeded Mills, just before the transition to the Canadian Alliance, he issued a thoughtful position paper calling for a greater Canadian engagement with the world. "Soft power" and "human security," which are increasingly adapted as United Nations goals, flow directly from the Canadian experience, particularly the Canadian experience in UN peacekeeping. It begins with the understanding that patrolling a ceasefire is only an interim step toward ending a conflict. The real end to war comes with the building of a normal, everyday life – a community life, in which citizens can expect to lead an orderly and largely peaceable existence. The 1980s and the 1990s brought a permanent shift – most conflict now is within nations, not between nations.

SATYA DAS

The old UN imperatives no longer work in this new world. The harsh proof came in the UN's futile and impotent efforts to patrol ceasefires in the Balkans, as the Yugoslavia held together by Marshal Tito fractured on the fault lines of lineage and blood. The "human security" agenda vigorously advocated by UN Secretary General Kofi Annan says, in essence, that in times of war, an individual or a community's human rights are the most important consideration. However Annan is constrained by his role in answering the question of whether these rights are more important than national sovereignty, the secretary-general has sought to balance respect for sovereignty with a robust advocacy of human security. This is a controversial view, and Canada has been one of Annan's strongest allies (along with the Netherlands, Norway and Sweden) and perhaps the most ardent champion. Axworthy and Robert Fowler, the former Canadian ambassador to the UN, now Ambassador to Italy, worked closely with Annan to push this concept in the face of the five permanent members of the Security Council, whose veto power was a principal reason during the Cold War for the world body's frequent inability to act swiftly and effectively. (While Security Council members have refrained from exercising the veto in the post-Soviet era, the potential exercise of a Security Council veto was the explanation advanced by the US and NATO for their decision to proceed unilaterally with the bombing of Serbia). With Axworthy's support, Fowler became Annan's surrogate voice on the Security Council. However the human security agenda develops, Axworthy can rightly take credit for putting it front and centre on the world stage.

Similarly, the concept of "soft power" is tied intimately to the new notions of building a peace and re-establishing a civil society in the wake of a conflict. Its critics misunderstood "soft power" to be a substitute for military might and the capacity for military intervention. Yet in its fuller sense, soft power is really about the peace-building capacity that is essential for any modern peacekeeping mission. It means that soldiers aren't enough to establish peace – you also need doctors, teachers, nurses, engineers, judges, civilian police, and garbage collectors. Rather than being a substitute for military force, "soft power" or the capacity to rebuild a civil society becomes a complementary partner to military-based peacekeeping, the component that gives peace a chance, after the soldiers are gone. There have been few happy examples where this has worked in practice rather than theory – East Timor is one, Cambodia might become another. Despite the failures like Sierra Leone and Congo, and the ambiguous outcome of the UN presence in Kosovo, it seems clear that there is a better chance peace can come from a combination of military and civil forces. Again, Axworthy can take due credit for an important Canadian role in developing and advancing the concept. "Axworthy challenged governments, foreign ministries, realist academics, and others to recognize the reality that individuals are often threatened and abused by their own governments," notes Steve Lee, director of the Canadian Centre for Foreign Policy Development. "There has been a re-think of sanctions, recognizing that sanctions often most affect women and children, far more than pariah world governments and leaders."

Axworthy laid the foundations of a 21st-century foreign policy, one that anticipates the turbulence of a world where the old East-West conflicts are gone, and one superpower reigns supreme. Of course, it is not evident whether and when a new East-West conflict might emerge. History will be a better judge of Axworthy's success than any contemporary opinions. No matter what fate awaits his effort to project the best of Canada as an example to the world, Axworthy is to be commended for making the effort, for playing the game so superbly, for giving new life to this country's animating dream – that we can build a better tomorrow for those who will follow us.

Yet Axworthy's efforts are just a beginning. The foundation he laid by introducing and entrenching the notion of human security demands continued Canadian leadership in sustaining peace. If the Aga Khan is right that we are a template of how cultural diversity ought to work, then we surely have an obligation to use the lessons we have learned from the experience of being Canadian, to assume the challenges of maintaining peace. The argument in the post-Cold War era – embraced in part by Annan and advanced aggressively by Canada – is that the protection of innocents comes first, human rights supersede all other concerns. The Canadian view holds that, ultimately, peacebuilding aims at building human security, a concept which includes democratic governance, human rights, and the rule of law, sustainable development, and equitable access to resources. Just as Canada was a pioneer in introducing and fine-tuning the notion of peacekeeping, so it must continue to be a leader in developing and implementing the concept of peacebuilding, in partnership with other like-minded and generally smaller nations. We can see too that the notion of human security and the need to put the lives of the innocent above the rights of state sovereignty, will become even more manifest in the aftermath of the 11 September 2001 attacks on New York and Washington. Once the US is fully re-engaged in the quest for global governance, there will be a greater need to transcend national boundaries to achieve human security. Using national borders will not be seen as a sufficient protection for terrorists who seek to hide from the consequences of their actions. By attacking US citizens directly as they went about their daily lives, the instigators unwittingly shattered the apathy and the complacency of the United States, and in the long run this may be the best catalyst for achieving sustainable peace in the world. The positive engagement of the United States in enabling a more just and equitable world order would be a reasonable outcome of a concerted global campaign to enhance human security. The US came to understand in the most tragic way that the pursuit of human security means taking all means necessary to assure the well-being of civilians. And in the global effort to eradicate terrorism, at last joined by the US, we may come to see the primacy of the idea that the safety of people is more important than recognising the sanctity of national borders.

The notion of sustainable peace isn't a theoretical conceit. It was forged in the cauldron of the decade-long civil wars that consumed the Balkans in the 1990s, as traditional UN roles of peacekeeping were tried and found wanting. When UN peacekeepers became helpless witnesses to genocide during a civil war, as Annan notes in his reference to Srebrenica, it was clear that the old notions of enforcing a cease-fire between adversaries couldn't suffice. Annan too has the United Nations system as a whole to focus as never before on peace-building – on action to identify and support structures that will strengthen and solidify peace. In the secretary-general's view, keeping peace in the sense of avoiding a relapse into armed conflict is a necessary but not sufficient condition for establishing the foundations of an enduring and just peace.

British Prime Minister Tony Blair hailed Kosovo as the first military intervention by the outside world to stop human rights violations against civilians. He saw it as a new frontier. (It should be noted though that Serbia saw this as a manifestation of neo-imperialism,

SATYA DAS

and other countries may well see international intervention as an unhappy return to the precepts and presumptions of the colonial era). But against the reality of entrenched Balkan hatred, just how far can the UN succeed? The counterpoint to that is to do nothing – and in today's world of borderless communications, there is little scope to do nothing, as horrifying images of faraway conflicts are rendered all too intimate and familiar by modern communications media. Taking some sort of effective action may seem like common sense, but it's much easier said than done. While the UN charter foresees intervention and by extension peacekeeping, there is no explicit provision for peace building. As the need for it evolves, the UN must develop the mechanisms and instruments necessary to engage Annan's broad notion of human security, and to make it a reality. The notion of creating civilian police, beginning a reconstruction of a ravaged society, creating civil authority, are all new areas of joint international endeavour in the aftermath of conflict. For a UN that has become accustomed to using soldiers to keep peace, the assembly of the military-civilian cohesion necessary to build peace is a monumental challenge.

This is a challenge Canada can and should embrace, if it is to fulfil its obligation as the world's best country to help establish a better future for humankind. We have been given a poignant and vivid example of how the necessary blend of soft power and hard power can work, in the public eulogy to the late Sgt. Marc Leger, one of four Canadian soldiers killed by an errant American bomb while on duty in Afghanistan in April 2002. When Leger was in Bosnia as a peacekeeper, he could not abide to simply prevent conflict – he went beyond his duty and his mandate to rebuild the basics of a normal life, to demand the necessary resources to rebuild a community. When he told the villagers they needed to elect a mayor and set up a civil administration, they wanted Leger to represent them. Yet Leger's extraordinary efforts merely underline a critical lack of the humanitarian and civilian resources that ought to accompany peacekeeping. We can start by building the civilian capacity essential to sustaining peace.

Whilst many countries have surplus soldiers, only a handful have paramilitary police. And few if any jurisdictions have a surplus of police whose main duty is to maintain peace and order within a given community. Even fewer nations or communities have a surplus of police officers, doctors, nurses, teachers, engineers, lawyers, waterworks builders, judges, civil administrators garbage collectors and other skilled personnel necessary to rebuild a normal life in a post-conflict society. Who will pay for extra police, nurses and the like? That's a key question as countries redefine peacekeeping. Would Canada and like-minded nations, for instance, allocate part of an enhanced peacebuilding budget to municipalities and provinces? And the key question, given the late 20th – and early 21st – century penchant in the industrialised world for lower taxes, is what would happen to that surplus civil capacity when it was not needed in the international arena – would taxpayers readily bear the cost?

Like an insurance policy, investing in peacebuilding helps to prevent future conflict, and in the particular case of Timor, it would provide the tools to enable the potentially oil-rich country to develop health care, education and the other building blocks of long-term peace and stability.

Yet this brings us back to the central question: Who will pay for peace? Even if the world assumes a collective responsibility, where will the money come from? How will it be distributed? And how much will be enough?

Equally important is the question of control. Should the UN distribute peace-building funds, or should it be done in some other way? Would the people who balk at paying $3 billion US to build East Timor anew continue to resist, even if the money was at hand, unless they had absolute say about how it were used?

Because this is uncharted territory for the United Nations, flexibility and accommodation become essential in collecting and delivering funds for peace building. It is surely an irony of our age that the very powers reluctant to fund the UN on grounds that it is inefficient or incompetent should be the ones who render it so. The streaks of exceptionalism and isolationism in the conduct of the foreign policy of the United States lead it to restrict or diminish funding for the United Nations. Yet it is the exercise of the Security Council veto by the US and the four other permanent members that has historically prevented the UN from swift, decisive, cohesive action with a broad and open-ended mandate. Inevitably, there will be conflict and controversy regarding the collection and disbursement of peace-building funds. A magnificent philanthropic gift like the $1 billion US donated by media magnate Ted Turner to the United Nations is a rare and happy event. Yet one magnanimous act is not enough, and it would be foolhardy to rely entirely on voluntary donations to build peace, and fund the necessities of post-conflict reconstruction. Civic-minded individuals and donor governments would have to give many billions more into a global fund, so that the investment revenue from that fund could pay for peacebuilding.

In seeking a workable solution, Canada can once again take the lead. Voluntary donations alone cannot work. The notion of a global facilities fund, as proposed in 1999 by scholars at the University of New York, relies too much on philanthropy and voluntarism. A more formal mechanism is vital to ensure long-term, stable funding. The most reliable instrument, if it can be implemented, might be a global tax on militarism. A legal framework would be a challenge to develop. One way to proceed might to build on the jurisdictional liberty offered to the International Criminal Court that Axworthy worked so hard to create. If criminal laws are applied internationally, can the same be done with certain civil laws, particularly relating to international trade and taxation? The danger, of course, is that an international tax on militarism might drive large portions of "defence spending" and the arms trade underground – and military spending into the grey areas of fluid government accounts.

Yet the absence of an international legal framework to permit global taxation of the legal portion of the arms trade need not be an insurmountable barrier. Countries like Canada, and the other vigorous champions of peace, might begin by "taxing" their own defence and military spending – by designating ten per cent of their military budgets specifically for a global peace-building fund. In Canada's case, this would come to an annual "tax" that would yield roughly four times as much money as Canada now pays in United Nations dues. NATO budgets taxed at that level would yield about $75 billion CDN a year. This would be entirely voluntary, but it would set an example. It would fit in well with the evolving "soft power" regime in international relations, because it would stand as a classical instance of using moral suasion to achieve a greater good.

If Canada and other military powers began to set aside parts of their own defence spending, and levied a special export tax on their arms manufactures, it would set an example for others. More practically, it would enable the beginning of what would end up as a permanent fund to enable peace-building and post-conflict reconstruction. There is little chance that it would yield the dividends of a full-fledged international tax on the arms trade. An initial target should be to raise enough to make the very idea of the tax credible – perhaps an amount as large as the annual budget for all other UN operations.

If one carries the castles-in-Spain thinking a step further, one can see that a viable international tax on the world's $1.5 trillion war spending could yield the revenues to fund peacebuilding. A relatively modest tax would bring substantial funds – taxing the arms trade and defence expenditure at five per cent, for instance, would also bring $75 billion CDN a year. That's a huge amount of money, considering that the UN budget for all its operations – from peacekeeping to development to health and children's services – is about one fifth that size. Taxing the arms trade and defence spending would be relatively straightforward, if a consensus were built to do so – the rationale being that the developed countries of the world, including the leading democracies, are the principal suppliers of arms that fuel conflict the world over. They are also the principal suppliers of peacekeepers, and of the meagre funds that are eventually used to build peace in the wake of these conflicts.

There is surely a sense of proportion and natural justice in the thought that those who provide the tools of war should pay to provide the tools of peace. Moreover, not all of this money would be poured into a conflict zone. A sizeable fund would enable the development of the civil capacity needed to build a peace. Funding would enable the creation of surplus civilian police, doctors, nurses, teachers, judges, engineers and so forth. Canada, for instance, might use a good portion of its contribution to global peace building to increase municipal budgets in Canada and other rich countries, so that municipalities would be able to develop surplus capacity that could then be channelled to post-conflict situations as the need arose. This capacity development in turn would enable rapid deployment of peace-builders, which could be assembled just as troops are for peace keeping.

Nonetheless, there remains the practical issue not just of tax collection, but of tax administration and disbursement. Who would control the fund? It is highly unlikely that the members of the United Nations would be content to see the funds administered by a third party beyond their control, even one as benign as the foundation set up to disburse Turner's largesse.

It is possible to foresee a United Nations-led or -mandated entity modelled on Britain's quangos (quasi autonomous governmental organisations) to gather and distribute a tax on the arms trade and defence spending. This agency or entity would effectively extend taxation influence, if not power, away from national governance to global governance. This would be a momentous step, which may be extremely difficult to attain – unless the post-September 11th climate can create a receptive consideration of such a scheme. Would the Security Council, particularly the P-5, entertain such a concept, particularly if the money initially came from voluntary taxation on the part of Canada and others?

One viable idea might be to extend a United Nations concept that has proven its worth, and its level of acceptability amongst both the General Assembly and the Security Council – a High Commission. It could work whether the global peace-building fund came from self-imposed taxes on defence spending by Canada and others, or from globally imposed taxes on the arms trade under a jurisdictional framework that has yet to be developed. A United Nations High Commissioner for Peace Building and Post-Conflict Reconstruction would provide the focal point that is so far lacking in global peace-building efforts. It would be a logical evolution of the UN system and the evolving UN role in implementing Annan's sweeping vision of human security and the protection of civilians in armed conflict.

A High Commissioner for Peace might be a necessary bridge between the military and civilian facets of peace-building and post-conflict reconstruction. The role might be particularly important in areas where there is a UN-sanctioned deployment rather than a UN-led deployment – as in the case of NATO's mandate in Bosnia and Herzegovina, or the initial Australian mandate in East Timor. A High Commissioner for Peace would use the surplus civil capacity generated by the fund to assemble peace-builders – Canadian nurses, Indian computer technicians, French paramilitary police, and the like. Because this would occur under the aegis of a UN high commission, there would in effect be a permanent General Assembly and Security Council authority, executed under the aegis of the Secretary General. This may not be ideal, in that countries in the past have refused to put troops under UN command and would not be particularly persuaded that a High Commissioner for Peace, who carries even less authority than the Secretary-General, ought to have troops at her disposal.

Yet a High Commissioner is not the only model, nor necessarily the most viable one. It might be simpler to begin, for instance, with a Special Representative of the United Nations Secretary General, appointed on a case-by-case basis. The Military Staff Committee of the UN already has the authority to handle troops, and that constitutional grounding in the UN Charter may in some cases make a Special Representative more palatable than a High Commissioner for Peace. Nonetheless, we need to think of ways to entrench a peace-sustenance consciousness. A vigorous debate about an expanded role for a peace-maintenance agency would be a valuable contribution.

The United Nations' August 2000 peacekeeping review stopped short of recommending a global ministry of defence, recommending instead that national governments and regional alliances prepare units of troops that might be readily deployed. Could such troops be at the disposal of a High Commissioner for Peace? If they were, their deployment might be more readily seen as part of a complex and on-going process of shaping a peace, rather than a military intervention that is not necessarily connected to other civil-society efforts. Certainly, the idea of putting UN troops directly under the aegis of a peace commissioner would send an important signal that the UN's longer-term goal is to craft a durable peace, rather than merely super-vising a ceasefire or the end of overt conflict.

Ironically, the development of a European standing army in October 2000, the most robust manifestation of the Franco-German entente that shaped post-war Europe, may provide the substance of a peace-building movement. The 60,000 strong force, nominally inde-pendent of NATO, could indeed be the basis of a rapid-deployment UN force. Canada has worked to give the UN a rapid reaction capa-bility – its 1995 report *Towards a Rapid Reaction Capability for the United Nations* was essentially means of projecting Canadian values into the realm of peace enforcement. Along with the Dutch and the Norwegians, Canada has long sought the development of an effective rapid deployment capability for the UN – one that could be seen as a necessary corollary to soft-power measures. If the European Union were to develop a corollary civil capacity, a peace-building and post-conflict reconstruction component, one could foresee a joint mili-tary-civil Canadian and European intervention force at the service of both NATO and the UN. This is precisely the sort of resource that would give a UN High Commissioner for Peace Building and Post-Conflict Reconstruction a strong foundation and bring legitimacy and credibility to international interventions.

The High Commissioner for Peace could work closely with the High Commissioner for Refugees and the High Commissioner for Human Rights in providing a comprehensive and coherent matrix for peace building and post-conflict reconstruction. The very creation of the office would send a strong signal about the international community's commitment to building peace. It would go a long way towards creating a more capable institutional framework to implement Annan's vision of human security. Moreover, since the purpose would be to encourage the development of the peace-building capacity within nations – as in Kosovo and Timor, bringing in outsiders only until the local population and indigenous resources are able to sustain a civil society based on peace and just governance – there is no question of these interventions being seen as a new tentative attempt at colonialism, nor as a neo-imperialist agenda entering by the back door.

Under the aegis of a UN High Commissioner for Peace, the international presence should be diverse and multilateral enough to banish any taint of imperialist intent. Yet the high commissioner's role is vital, if outside aid and indigenous resources are to mesh effectively and well. One of the gaps in the present climate is the absence of widespread integration between the hard-power and soft-power options. Military intervention and humanitarian assistance often exist in a post-conflict intervention, and indeed both are necessary to achieve stability and lay a foundation for post-conflict reconstruction.

The Canadian military, for instance, is among the first to recognise that finding the ideal blend of hard power and soft power will become the principal challenge of future peace-building interventions: soldiers and civilians working in a co-ordinated manner to achieve the same objectives. The events in Afghanistan in the spring of 2002 offered a vivid illustration. Even as Canadian commandos from Joint Task Force 2 scoured the mountains for the remnants of the Taliban, even as Canadian soldiers from Princess Patricia's Canadian Light Infantry fought side by side with Americans against al Qaeda soldiers in mountain caves, the interim government of Hamid Karzai enlisted the help of the United Nations and its agencies to begin restoring the normal intercourse of civilian life. In March 2002, International Women's Day was celebrated for the first time by thousands of Afghanis who were able to shed the head-to-toe covering demanded by the Taliban regime, a symbolic reclamation of a life free of terror. The reconstruction aid promised to Karzai, the international efforts to ward off starvation in the aftermath of the civil war, were all seen as necessary steps in rebuilding civil society – as necessary as ensuring that the Taliban and al Qaeda could not regroup and return.

By establishing a High Commissioner for Peace, the UN might create the institutional framework to blend hard power and soft power, bringing together expert practitioners of each option. The evolution of peace building and the necessity for post-conflict reconstruction require new ideas and new approaches. A stable and permanent global fund built by a tax on defence spending and the arms trade, and a UN high commissioner to make use of that fund, are logical extensions of Annan's bold strides towards making human security the very *raison d'être* of the United Nations.

When Axworthy first began charting the unexplored territory of "soft power" in international relations, it wasn't all that easy to see how it might be applied. The core ideas of soft power – using moral leadership rather than economic or military might to achieve one's goals – seemed to flow from the Canadian desire to do good in a bad world. Yet with far too many instances of hard power – the bombs and the money, if you like – winning the day, it wasn't clear where moral suasion might lead. Would it be simply another expression of Canadian idealism, or would it be workable enough to achieve tangible results? Axworthy's early successes boded well. Against quite long odds, the convention to control land mines became international law after the number of countries that ratified surpassed the threshold of 60. The idea of an international court of justice was another laudable step.

But then Prime Minister Jean Chrétien's government was thrust into a war of aggression against Serbia, bypassing the United Nations that Canada had so resolutely supported over the decades. Chrétien was given less than an evening to decide: Are you for us or against us, asked the hard-power specialists at NATO. Once again, it seemed, hard power won the day. Axworthy and Chrétien tried to put a brave face on it, saying that the NATO campaign was meant ultimately to uphold human security, thereby using military force to attain a laudable goal, to end the killing of Albanians in Kosovo by the forces of Slobodan Milosevic. It was a good try, even though it wasn't entirely convincing. It was less convincing when the rampaging thugs of the Serbian military survived more or less intact, the Communist tyrant Milosevic remained in power, and millions of ordinary Serbs faced a winter without heat and power. And all conviction faded when the rampaging thugs of the so-called Kosovo Liberation Army started to tally up their own score of murder and mayhem against the Serbs that remained in the rebel province. The Balkans clearly displays the limits of hard power. Military intervention stopped most (but certainly not all) of the killing, and an international military presence will help to maintain a semblance of order and stability. The overthrow of Milosevic – and the astonishment of seeing him tried by an international court for crimes against humanity – may have had as much to do with luck as with design. Yet the very fact that Milosevic was made to answer charges against him (and his singular defence that it's all lies), and had a chance in turn to defend himself by accusing NATO and the outside world of crimes against his people, shows that soft power concepts can indeed be made to work.

Hard power alone cannot create or build a sustainable peace. That is the task of soft power: creating and nourishing civil society. Yet we must recognise that civil society cannot be created in a climate of violence, imminent war, a tenuous ceasefire and incipient chaos. That is why the challenge of blending hard power and soft power – enforcing by military or policing presence the rule of law so that civil society can be rebuilt – is a fundamental challenge in global governance. The elements of civil society must be established before anyone can talk of true stability. The rule of law, representative government, the assurance of fundamental human rights, broad access to education and health care, are the foundations of any lasting peace. Representative government should by its definition include an element of democracy, but in many war-ravaged regions, the guarantee of human rights may be a more important factor in building peace. Given these conditions, a working democracy can evolve from the other elements of civil society. The Balkans, therefore, can become a proving ground for soft power. So too can Indonesia, and its newly independent enclave, East Timor. Can civil society be built in these places where evil was done? Understanding that an affirmative answer is the best way to guarantee peace, Canada can lead the international community in laying the foundations of civil society in those countries. The aftermath of civil war may in fact be the best time to engage in peace building. The application of soft power ought to begin in the post-war rebuilding – and in the case of Indonesia, in the post-dictatorship rebuilding.

Canada has a great deal of experience and expertise in building strong civil institutions. It is a hidden strength, never fully exploited. But our ability to craft a society based on peace, order and good governance makes the Canadian experience particularly valuable in countries seeking a new future. Canada will find a receptive audience, whether in Indonesia, which realized belatedly that economic miracles would ultimately collapse unless they are based on the rule of law, or the Balkans, which must finally see that war only begets more war. The other attraction of soft-power solutions to conflict is that they carry a much cheaper price tag than war. Education and health care are relatively low cost investments, but they pay enormous dividends in enabling the growth and development of a society. Establishing the rule of law, too, can be relatively painless if it is done while an international peacekeeping force is at hand.

Hard power cannot achieve a comprehensive peace by itself. But soft power cannot create the basic conditions in which a peace can be built. Combining the strengths of both options, in the Balkans and in East Timor, might create the most enduring peace of all. Had it not been for those experiences – and the UN success in restoring elected governance to Cambodia – the entire intervention in Afghanistan might have taken quite a different turn. In effect, peacekeeping becomes a way of enforcing stability while civil society is under construction. With ample experience in both, Canada should lead in developing new ways to keep and build a sustainable peace. If we can even engage in a determined effort, we will begin to fulfil our obligation to lead the future, because we will give back to the world some of the ennobling human experiences that came together in our national space to make Canada the best country.

Why Canada Will
Lead the Future

The case for Canadian global leadership might have remained a fanciful theory, if the United States had continued to see its manifest destiny as being the world's sole superpower. That has changed in the aftermath of the terrorist attacks. In the fall of 2001, there was a palpable sense of self-examination and re-evaluation, an effort to answer the "Why" of the brazen assault upon the symbols of US power.

And in that search for a "why," there is indeed a possibility that Canada's influence and example will have greater relevance than ever before. To understand why there is a chance to turn *The Best Country's* idealism into concrete action, come with me to a hotel ballroom in Dallas, Texas on 28 November 2001. Outside, among the sterile streetscape of towers and parkades – with not even a shop or retail business in sight – a chill wind blows freezing rain through the downtown canyons. Inside, several hundred members of Dallas's elite mingle with Western Canadians. This is the gala lunch of the Team Canada West trade mission. In normal circumstances, this first-of-a-kind trip would offer a chance to talk deals and make deals. Yet in the weeks after the terrorist attacks, the times are anything but normal.

The tables are set with china and silver. Even the banquet chairs are draped in elegant cloth tied with a gold ribbon. Texas Governor Rick Perry is approaching the stage. His predecessor is now the President of the United States. Perry looks tanned, handsome and at ease – yet anyone with a cursory knowledge of US politics would know that it takes a remarkable combination of connections and ambition to rise to the governor's chair in Texas. Yet today, Perry is about to rise above the cut-and-thrust of political life. He has just listened to an eloquent and emotional speech from Paul Celucci, the former Massachusetts governor who is the US ambassador to Canada. Celucci tells the Texas audience how Canada has proven to be the truest friend of the United States in its time of grief – how quickly Canada acted to accommodate diverted US flights on September 11, and about the rally on Parliament Hill that brought an astonishing show of support for the US. He heaps praise on Prime Minister Jean Chrétien, who looks embarrassed, and with his body language offers an "it was no big deal" gesture to Celucci.

Perry will not let it go, when he begins to speak. His voice breaking, pausing five times to control his emotions and regain his composure, in a slow and deliberate voice with an enunciation far clearer than Chrétien ever musters, Perry quoted every word of the Prime Minister's speech on Parliament Hill on 14 September, when 100,000 Canadians gathered to show solidarity with the United States: "Let me tell you what this man said," he begins.

> You have assembled before you, here on Parliament Hill and right across Canada, a people united in outrage, in grief, in compassion, and in resolve. A people of every faith and nationality to be found on earth. A

people who, as a result of the atrocity committed against the United States on September 11, 2001, feel not only like neighbours. But like family. At a time like this, words fail us. We reel before the blunt and terrible reality of the evil we have just witnessed. We cannot stop the tears of grief. We cannot bring back lost wives and husbands. Sons and daughters. American citizens, Canadian citizens, citizens from all over the world. We cannot restore futures that have been cut terribly short. At a time like this, the only saving grace is our common humanity and decency. At a time like this, it is our feelings, our prayers and our actions that count. By their outpouring of concern, sympathy and help, the feelings and actions of Canadians have been clear. And, even as we grieve our own losses, the message they send to the American people is equally clear. Do not despair. You are not alone. We are with you. The whole world is with you. The great Martin Luther King, in describing times of trial and tribulation, once said that: "In the end, it is not the words of your enemies that you remember, it is the silence of your friends.

Mr. Ambassador, as your fellow Americans grieve and rebuild, there will be no silence from Canada. Our friendship has no limit. Generation after generation, we have travelled many difficult miles together. Side by side, we have lived through many dark times. Always firm in our shared resolve to vanquish any threat to freedom and justice. And together, with our allies, we will defy and defeat the threat that terrorism poses to all civilized nations. Mr. Ambassador, we will be with the United States every step of the way. As friends. As neighbours. As family.

"That's what this man said, ladies and gentlemen," Perry said. "This man right here. That's what he said, 'our friendship has no limit.' We are with you. As family."

There were tears in the eyes of each of the five Americans at my table. The Texan to my right, an energy company executive, turned to me, shook my hand and said, "Thank you for being with us. Thank you."

The emotion in that room, the sense of gratitude, of fellow-feeling, became altogether overwhelming. "You're truly our best friends, and we never get a chance to say that," said the marketing professor to my left. "I'm saying it now. Thank you for standing with us. We'll never forget what you've done for us. Never."

When Chrétien finally approached the podium, his every move shown on two giant screens, there was an astonishing air of anticipation. "He looks like a leader," said the marketing professor. "You look at him and you know he can lead a great country."

Sensing the occasion, Chrétien elevated a fairly standard business-audience speech to something befitting a sense of communion. For once, the Prime Minister was an orator, and when he spoke of the relationship between the two countries, he invested his words with such authenticity of feeling that the people at my table and surrounding ones sat spellbound: "Historians have pointed out that the American Revolution created not one, but two countries. We took separate political roads and we have had our differences. But over the generations, we have built a partnership of unmatched respect, civility and openness. Freedom and justice are our birthright and our common cause. We understand that freedom is the source of human dignity and fulfillment," Chrétien said to hushed ballroom. "And on a personal note, I want to tell this audience how proud all Americans can be of the leadership of a great Texan: President George Bush. In our many meetings and discussions since September 11th, I have been deeply impressed by his resolve. On behalf of the people of Canada, I offer him our support. The President and I also both understand the broader threat posed by terrorism. For most of our history, we in North America have been fortunate to live in peace, untouched by attack. That has changed. But we must never forget that the ultimate goal of terrorists is not to capture us by the force of arms. But by the force of terror. They don't want to occupy us. They want to shut us down! Ladies and gentlemen, Canada and the United States will never let this happen!"

At that moment, I felt that the 1,100 people in the room would have followed Chrétien anywhere. And when he spoke at last of economic opportunity in Canada, it seemed not only a sales pitch but also a natural extension of the friendship: "The same innovative and pioneering spirit that is a trademark of Texas is in full vigour throughout Western Canada. Where Canadians are working together to build on our incredible wealth in natural resources, to develop new expertise in information and communications technologies and create an advanced, diversified 21st century economy. Team Canada West features representatives of 60 companies from all sectors of the Western Canadian economy. Many of these companies are leaders in their fields, not just in Canada but globally. . . . They are looking for new partners, new customers and new investors. They want you to think of

Western Canada when you are looking for cutting-edge ideas and infrastructure."

And there was even a rumbling of assent from the audience, a who's-who of robust champions of free-market capitalism, when Chrétien said: "Addressing the problems of the developing world will also continue to be a Canadian priority. Advanced industrial nations have both a moral obligation to – and an economic interest in – increasing their development assistance. The Government of Canada will fulfil that obligation."

The following night, 29 November 2001, the same Canadians are in Los Angeles with a different cast of Americans. We are at the Getty Center, the grand hilltop museum that houses the world's greatest private collection of Greco-Roman art. It's a showy evening, with a cast of power brokers from the world of entertainment and technology – Jack Valenti from the movie industry, an assortment of Hollywood film stars and singers, Canadian expatriates. There's a concert led by the Canadian composer David Foster, Paul Anka, Chantal Kreviazuk. The Americans there make a point of personally thanking the Canadians they meet, for standing with the United States in the aftermath of September 11. The "news story" from earlier in the day is about Hollywood's complaints about Canada "stealing" movie business away. Yet that night, there's no talk of the dispute. Three hundred Canadian voices join five hundred American ones in singing Foster's evocative arrangement of *God Bless America*, and as soon as the song is done, the emotion is as tangible as it was in Dallas – an absolute sense of fellow-feeling, of belonging, of the human currents that run beneath the politics, economics and borders. This US receptiveness to Canada, the easy acceptance of Canadians as "family" gives us both credibility and influence in individual and collective engagements with our American neighbours. It is difficult to imagine a rights-based approach, and a human security agenda, flourishing on a global scale without some degree of interest and support from the United States. Can we bring the Americans with us as we move forward with an expansion of the meaning and possibility of globalisation? Perhaps we can, if we use this new opening to make the United States the leading export market for Canada's model civil society, and the elements of the "kinder gentler nation" the US yearned to become.

As I argued in the opening chapter, the world view of the United States arose from the marriage of robust military power and the forces of rampant capitalism – a marriage undone by the twin shocks of the 11 September 2001 attacks and the collapse of the energy trader Enron. Lawrence Summers, US Secretary of the Treasury during the Clinton presidency, succinctly set out the American view in an October 1999 speech to the Democratic Leadership Annual Conference in Washington: "The crucial link between closer economic integration and our national security is this: we are much less likely as a nation to be drawn into conflict if nations of the world are strong, and are forging ever closer connections, than if they are financially unstable and disconnected. In short, trade promotes prosperity and by promoting prosperity, promotes peace. . . . Trade, then, is the pursuit of peace by other means. But we should never forget that it is also the pursuit of higher living standards for Americans. To put it bluntly: even if closer integration did not help to make America a safer nation, we would still want to support it because it helps make us a more prosperous one."

Summers spelled out what this means: "As we move to a more truly global and integrated economy, and as capital becomes so much more mobile than labor, there are legitimate concerns that companies will exploit that greater mobility by playing off competing jurisdictions against one an other. The fear is that we will find ourselves in a race to the bottom – a bottom in which governments cannot promote fair taxes, uphold fair labor standards, protect the environment or promote other key American values. That is not the world we want to build. And it is not the world that we are building. Just as national regulations and standards evolved in the United States in the last century in response to the consequences of inter-state competition – so international agreements and institutions will be needed to provide an enduring basis for integration at the international level."

Summers gave utterance to a broader and more inclusive view of economic globalisation, than the one practiced by the Enrons of the world. Yet that view was seldom articulated, let alone acted upon, in the last two decades of the 20th century. The pendulum swung far towards deregulation, privatisation, the view that government should be subservient to the needs of business. Above all, the doctrine of both Bush *père* and Bush *fils* embraced the blind faith that the unchecked pursuit of economic gain and the triumph of individualism is a substitute for a collective sense of belonging in which notions of the Common Good and the Common Wealth motivate and empower citizens to shape their common future. The advent of terrorism on American soil finally brought an understanding that in essence, terrorists are nourished in the vacuum left by the absence of democratic governance, civil society, social justice and economic opportunity. Canada's model of civil society offers the antithesis – the model of how the world can co-operate and coexist. And it is as important to present this view in the US as it is in the developing world. America's imperial hubris has been dealt a blow, but it has not disappeared. If it can be tempered with Canadian modesty, we will indeed have a chance to craft a better world.

While the United States represents a promising opportunity to project Canadian values and the Canadian model of civil society, it is by no means the only one. Canada already exports democratic governance, transparency, accountability and other tools of governance informed with Canadian values. The Alberta-Mpumalanga Governance Project, for instance, aims to help South Africa and its sub-national governments formulate a new constitution and move to a federal system through sharing governmental decision-making structures and processes. The project involves everything from economic development policy, business planning, financial management and accountability, to teenage street prostitution and the problems facing disadvantaged youth. It is not the only such project. The Canadian International Development Agency funds dozens of projects aimed at enhancing civil society in many parts of the world. Canada has a privileged relationship with the four nations that will form the dominant economic forces of the next decades. As we noted in the first chapter, the world's largest economic powers are the US, China, Japan and India. It is surely a worthy Canadian ambition to engage and influence these partners, in moving towards a culture of peace based on the new notions of human security. And if we choose to embark on the course of leadership, we should do so with the confidence that we are not alone. There are like-minded countries, like-minded peoples, like-minded individuals in every society and state who would join us in our quest to project Canadian values, to invest real meaning in peace, freedom and justice.

M.K. Gandhi set out the path in the first decades of the 20th century, when he described the world that waited to be built:

"Perhaps never before has there been so much speculation about the future as there is today. Will our world always be one of violence? Will there always be poverty, starvation, misery? Will we have a firmer and wide belief in religion, or will the world be godless? If there is to be a great change in society, how will that change be wrought? By war, or revolution? Or will it come peacefully? Different men give different answers to these questions, each man drawing the plan of tomorrow's world as he hopes and wishes it to be. I answer not only out of belief but out of conviction. The world of tomorrow will be, must be, a society based on non-violence. That is the first law; out of it all other blessings will flow. It may seem a distant goal, an impractical Utopia. But it is not in the least unobtainable, since it can be worked for here and now. An individual can adopt the way of life of the future – the non-violent way – without having to wait for others to do so. And if an individual can do it, cannot whole groups of individuals? Whole nations? Men often hesitate to make a beginning because they feel that the objective cannot be achieved in its entirety. This attitude of mind is precisely our greatest obstacle to progress – an obstacle that each man, if he only will it, can clear away."

It is within us, as Canadians, to strive towards Gandhi's ideal. As the best country in the world, we have made a fine beginning. If we have the audacity and determination to share what is best in us, we shall indeed fulfil Laurier's prophecy, and come to fill the 21st century.

Endnotes

1 The United Nations notes that the Human Development Index (HDI) measures a country's achievements in three aspects of human development: longevity, knowledge, and a decent standard of living. Longevity is measured by life expectancy at birth; knowledge is measured by a combination of the adult literacy rate and the combined gross primary, secondary, and tertiary enrolment ratio; and standard of living, as measured by national income.

The HDI is not enough to measure a country's level of development, however. The concept of human development is much broader than can be captured in the HDI. The HDI, for example, does not reflect political participation or gender inequalities. Measuring human poverty in the richest countries shows surprising results. The United States, with the highest GDP per capita, also has the highest extent of deprivations. The indices can only offer a broad proxy on the issues of human development, gender, and human poverty. A fuller picture of a country's level of human development requires analysis of other human development indicators and information.

National income as measured by Gross Domestic Product (GDP) cannot be used to measure human development instead of the HDI, as GDP per capita only reflects average national income. It tells nothing of how that income is distributed. And it tells nothing of how that income is spent – whether it is spent on universal health and education or for military expenditures. Comparing GDP per capita and HDI can reveal much about national policy choices. For example, a country with a very high GDP per capita such as Qatar has a lower HDI rank because of a lower level of educational attainment. Antigua and Barbuda have roughly half the GDP per capita of Qatar but have a higher HDI rank.

The human development index (HDI) attempts to make an assessment of 174 very diverse countries, with very different price levels. To do so it uses Purchasing Power Parity (PPP) to account for price differences between countries and therefore better reflects people's living standards. In theory, at the rate, one PPP dollar has the same purchasing power in the domestic economy as one US dollar has in the US economy.

2   **Human Development Index Ranking, 2000**
    1 Canada
    2 Norway
    3 United States
    4 Australia
    5 Iceland
    6 Sweden
    7 Belgium
    8Netherlands
    9 Japan
    10 United Kingdom
Human Development Index ranking, 2001
    1 Norway
    2 Australia

3 Canada

4 Sweden

5 Belgium

6 United States

7 Iceland

8 Netherlands

9 Japan

10 Finland

2000 Ranking of World Economies (PPP)

1 United States

2 China

3 Japan

4 India

5 Germany

6 France

7 United Kingdom

8 Italy

9 Brazil

10 Russian Federation

11 Mexico

12 Canada

3 In the 1871 Census of Canada, British and French origins dominated the population of 3,485,761 according to the Historical
Statistics of Canada, published in 1983 by Statistics Canada.
While there were 2.11 million Britons and 1.32 million French,
there were only four Canadians of Chinese origin. By the 1881
census, the number of "Asiatic" Canadians increased from four a
decade earlier to 4,383. By the 1901 census there were 23,731 in

the "Asiatic" category, growing to 43,213 by 1911 – by which time Canada's population grew to 7.2 million. By 1921, in a Canadian population of 8.8 million, there were 65,914 Asiatics. The Asiatic population peaked at 84,548 in the 1931 census, before beginning decades of decline provoked by the Chinese head tax and the later exclusion acts. The "Asiatic" population began to increase again in the 1950s, and by the 1961 census 121,753. In the 1996 census, 1.97 million Canadians identified themselves as being of Asian origin, compared with 3.27 million of British Isles origin and 2.68 million of French origin. By comparison, 10.22 million residents identified themselves as being of mixed blood or "multiple origins" while 5.33 million refused to categorize themselves by race or ethnicity, choosing to be grouped under "Canadian origins."

4 For example, in Alberta, manufacturing is No. 1 source of GDP, having taken over from resource extraction in 1997, even though the manufacturing sector is still behind processing of natural resources.

5 From *Mon Pays* by Gilles Vigneault, translated by Satya Das

6 Statistics Canada ethnic origins, 1996 Census: Winnipeg, British and French single origins 83,955 and total population 660,055 (12.72 per cent); Calgary, 106,750 British and French of 815,985 (13.08 per cent); Edmonton 96,695 British and French of 854,225 population (11.32 per cent); Vancouver 244,605 British and French of 1,813,935 total population (13.48 per cent). Data at:
http://www.statcan.ca/english/Pgdb/People/Population/demo28h.htm

SATYA DAS is an experienced opinion leader; a pioneer in defining and advocating Canadian values; a noted analyst of political, economic, social and cultural issues. Satya served on the Editorial Board of *The Edmonton Journal* for more than a dozen years, and travelled widely as a foreign correspondent. He was born in India, and emigrated to Canada with his parents when he was 12. Satya and his wife Mita have two school-aged daughters.

He has received the following major awards: Citation of Merit for Editorial Writing, National Newspaper Awards 1996; Media Human Rights Award, League for Human Rights of B'nai Brith Canada 1998; The Alberta Human Rights Award, for leadership in advancing human rights in Alberta, Province of Alberta 1999; Citation Award, for lifetime services to human rights and culture, City of Edmonton Salute to Excellence, 2001.

Satya's previous book, *Dispatches from a Borderless World*, published by NeWest Press, was named one of the top 10 books of 1999 by the Edmonton Public Library.